THE 32-GUN FRIGATE
ESSEX

THE 32-GUN FRIGATE

ESSEX

CONWAY MARITIME PRESS

Portia Takakjian

Frontispiece
1. 'Essex, American Frigate'. Watercolour attributed to Joseph Howard. *The Peabody Museum of Salem*

© Portia Takakjian, 1990

First published in 1990 by Conway Maritime Press

This edition published in 2005 by
Conway Maritime Press
The Chrysalis Building
Bramley Road
London W10 6SP
www.conwaymaritime.com

An imprint of **Chrysalis** Books Group plc

ISBN 1 84486 013 2

A CIP catalogue record for this book is available from the British Library

Printed and bound in Singapore

CONTENTS

ACKNOWLEDGEMENTS

I would like to extend special thanks to the following individuals for their generous assistance: Mr William W Jeffries, Mr James W Cheevers, Mr Robert F Sumrall of the United States Naval Academy Museum, for research assistance; Commander Kenneth A Johnson, for locating critical material on armament changes for the *Essex*, and for reviewing the service record; Mr Richard L Eddy for suggestions and reviewing the manuscript; Mr David C Roach, for locating obscure research material, and to my two sons who have supported the *Essex* project from its beginnings in 1975.

INTRODUCTION

The aftermath of the Revolution was a time of great political and economic difficulty for the United States. The most serious threat to the new nation's trade came from an unexpected source: the pirate Barbary states of North Africa.

Economic chaos dictated the sale of the remaining ships of the Continental Navy, while unprotected ships and seamen fell prey to the Dey of Algiers. Despite the raids by the Barbary pirates in 1785, Congress could not raise support for a permanent army or naval force. As attacks on shipping escalated, suggestions were made to comply with the demands of the Dey for tribute or to subsidize a European power to protect American trade.

Portugal's blockade of the Straits of Gibraltar had confined the Dey's activities to the Mediterranean until October 1793, when a twelve-month truce was established and Portugal lifted her blockade. Only then did Congress decide to protect American shipping by authorizing the construction of six frigates with a law passed on 27 March 1794.

Depredations upon United States' shipping and merchant seamen were not the only spur to action by the Congress. Attempts at neutrality in conflicts between the Dutch, British and French had proven futile. Without a navy to protect their interests, merchants in the United States were subject to soaring insurance costs, while at the same time losing ships and their cargoes; these merchants applied considerable pressure upon Congress for relief.

Despite the peace treaty signed with Algiers in September 1795, Congress authorized the construction of three of the original six frigates, the *United States*, the *Constitution* and the *Constellation*. In November of the following year Congress suspended construction after an unsatisfactory peace was signed with the Pasha of Tripoli.

The undeclared war with France was a direct result of the Jay Treaty, signed in 1794, and the notorious XYZ Affair in which France sought tribute for the protection of US shipping. Congress responded by the establishment of a naval department, and President Adams appointed Benjamin Stoddart as the first Secretary of the Navy on 18 May 1798. In April of that year Congress had authorized Adams to build, hire or purchase twelve ships, each to carry up to twenty-two guns. By an Act of 30 June 1798 the Navy Department encouraged the building, by subscription, of warships by private builders. Now Congress authorized the construction of the remaining three of the six original frigates of 1794, the *President*, the *Congress* and the *Chesapeake*.

In August of 1798 the subscription begun by the Salem merchants in June began to have an effect. The correspondence between the Senator from Massachusetts, Benjamin Goodhue, and the Secretary of State Timothy Pinkering reveal behind-the-scenes manoeuvres that would make Salem the building site for one of the proposed frigates. On 9 October, Benjamin Goodhue received a reply from Secretary of the Navy Stoddart confirming the building of the frigate *Essex*, and outlining the procedures required from either the frigate committee or the appointed agent. Selection of the builder and designer would be left to the agent or committee. They would also be allowed to select the men and officers to command the ship. The first order of business after the committee had been formed was the selection of William Hackett as the designer and superintendent of construction, followed by Enos Briggs as the builder.

William Hackett was born on 1 May 1739, one of four sons of William and Elizabeth Hackett. As a boy, until the age of twelve, he was employed in his father's shipyard at Salisbury, Massachusetts. After his father's death he moved on to other local yards. His name is linked with those of his cousin James 'Major' Hackett and his uncle, John Hackett, both shipbuilders in their own right. The seemingly military title of Major related to the hierarchy within the shipbuilding community; William was given the rank of Lieutenant at Lake George, where he was overseer of carpenters in 1759 while building the *Radeau* during the French and Indian wars, and his cousin James was ranked as Major while at John Langdon's shipyard at Portsmouth, New Hampshire, during the building of the Continental frigate *Raleigh*. Local militia men retained these ranks throughout their lifetimes, but it was William's association with his cousin James in joint building projects which caused the confusion between them in the attribution of the building and design of particular vessels. It is generally accepted that William was responsible for the designs of several Revolutionary War vessels including the brigantine *Massachusetts*, the sloop of war *Tyrannicide* (built at Salisbury in 1776), the sloop of war *Ranger* (built at Portsmouth NH in 1777 by his cousin James), the 74-gun ship *America* (also at Portsmouth and presented to the French government), and the Continental frigate *Alliance* (built in 1778 by his uncle John at Salisbury). After the Revolution he was engaged in design and construction, notably of the 600-ton merchantman *Massachusetts* launched at Quincy in 1789.

After this period little is known of his activities until 1794, when he is mentioned in a letter from the Secretary of War Henry Knox to Henry Jackson, the Navy Agent in Boston. By this time William was 55 years old, and it seems odd that the Secretary should have mentioned the name of his uncle John, who by then must have been well into his seventies, as the constructor for the *Constitution*. An extract from the letter follows:

Sir,

I am desirous that Mr John Hackett near Newbury Port who built the *Alliance* frigate during the late war should be engaged as constructor of the forty-four gun ship to be built at Boston — It is understood that there are three Hacketts, one of whom, named William, I believe, and is subject to temporary insanity — you will not engage. This point must be well ascertained.

Whether or not William was at this time confused with his cousin James is not known, but the stigma of this remark has been attached to William Hackett and his work on the draught of the *Essex* from that day forward.

The last ship designed and built by William Hackett was the 190-ton ship *Caroline* at Portsmouth launched in December 1800.

THE DESIGN

The controversy surrounding the draught of the *Essex* by William Hackett has been due, in part, to what some consider its unpolished state, questionable draughtsmanship and confusing lines. Enlargements of the photographic copies from the National Archives have done little to correct this image. On these copies most of the delicate pencil lines delineating the curved sweeps for the gunports, buttuck lines and diagonals, and the erasures and corrections which would contribute to a better understanding of the inked lines, are, for the most part, lost. Further efforts to create a so-called line copy from Hackett's shaded pencil and ink drawing render the design even more obscure. Despite this drawback, these line copies do serve a purpose: when enlarged, they reveal dramatically the significant notations made by Hackett. These are neither random nor arbitrary jottings; each has a distinct meaning. They offer us the unique opportunity to observe, at first hand, the eighteenth century design and construction techniques used by Hackett, and allow us to trace the designer's steps as his work on the *Essex* lines progressed. The following discussion of Hackett's design and its evolution can best be understood by reference to the draught and annotations reproduced on p26 below.

A clear understanding of this draught is essential to an understanding of the design of the ship herself; it is therefore important to decipher Hackett's notations and calculations and to find the probable sources for the proportions and rules he observed. The idea that American shipbuilders and designers existed in a kind of vacuum untouched by the design principles of their European cousins can be disproven by the weight of evidence to the contrary in the case of William Hackett and his lines for the *Essex* (see Table 2).

While it is possible that William Hackett worked by tradition and experience, there is strong evidence to suggest that he had access to tables of scantling, either transcribed from published works or the works themselves. It appears to be more than a coincidence that his proportions and dimensions match those from two major sources, *The Shipbuilder's Repository* of 1789, and Steel's *Shipwright's Vade Mecum* of 1805, a compendium of earlier published material with some revisions in the tables. These are of particular interest because both provide insight into the proportions which guided Hackett during the design, and cast light on the interesting question of how he arrived at the length of his gun deck and the distance between the fore and aft perpendiculars.

There is clear evidence that Hackett's draught is a working drawing, and something of his method is revealed within it. Two features of the draught are particularly informative: the framework of his station lines and the implications of his annotations and calculations.

The broadly spaced station lines on the draught include space for three

TABLE 1: DIMENSIONS

	Hackett draught		12 December 1799 William Hackett (Superintendent) Enos Briggs (Constructor)		1807–8 Josiah Fox	
	ft	in	ft	in	ft	in
Length of gun deck	141		141		141	
Payable length of keel	118		118		118	
Breadth of beam for tonnage	37		37		37	
Depth of hold	12	3	12	3	12	3
Height between decks (gun & lower)	5	10	5	9	5	9
Height under quarterdeck forward			6	3	6	3
Height under quarterdeck aft			6	6		
Height forecastle			6	2		
Height waist	6				6	
Length of quarterdeck			70			
Length of forecastle			34			
Deadrise*		(27)				27
Tonnage**					850²¹/₉₅ tons	

* Deadrise is not listed in the dimensions on Hackett's draught but is measured on the body plan.
** Tonnage noted on Joseph Waters' abstract of costs for the *Essex*.

intermediate frame bends marked by two short perpendiculars. Their placement between the fore and aft perpendiculars is based on the total number of feet in the fore and after bodies from the table. Forward of midships, these station lines are carried as far as station S and traces of faint pencil lines carry them still further to what would be the position of station X. Aft of midships, the stations are carried to number 30, although Hackett intended to bring them to 33, which is shown as the last station on his body plan. Each of the stations has been numbered and lettered along the top edge of the keel. There is no 'deadflat' in the true sense, but still Hackett has marked this area with repetitive numbers and letters to extend the waist.

This theoretical framework would serve, among other things, to work out the framing system and assist in determining the amount of timber required to build the frame bends. To this end, Hackett had to calculate the number of single frames between the fore and aft perpendiculars, and the number outside these limits. This brings us to the two groups of calculations located to the right of his scale below the sheer plan on the draught. These focus on his efforts to establish the final location of all the frame bends. He begins with preparatory calculations based on the fore and after bodies from the tables with a theoretical width of 2.22ft for each frame space, as follows:

Preparatory Calculations

1. Width of theoretical frame space 2.22ft, x number of spaces (54) on draught = 119.88ft (120ft allocated for square frame bends)
2. LBP 139.9ft, less 119.88ft = 20.02ft = number of feet for all cants
3. 20.02ft divided by two thirds for number of feet for fore and one third for aft cants
   = 6.67ft aft cants, 13.34ft fore cants
4. The number of feet divided by the frame space gives the number of frames fore and aft
   6.67 ÷ 2.22 = 3 frame spaces aft (measured to the fore side of the sternpost at the keel)
   13.34 ÷ 2.22 = 6 frame spaces forward (measured to the aft side of the stem at the height of the gun deck).

TABLE 2: **SOURCES OF DIMENSIONS AND PROPORTIONS**

	Dimensions		Proportions	Source	Remarks
	ft	in			
Length of the gun deck	140	0		Table of scantling, *Shipbuilder's Repository*, 1789	Parallel to the keel at the height of the wing transom from aft side of rabbet of the stern to fore side of rabbet of stem
Depth of the keel	1	6		Table of scantling, Steel's *Shipwright's Vade Mecum* 1805 **	Includes 2in for rabbet of keel. See Briggs for timber 23 November 1798: 146ft, 16in square in four pieces
Siding of the keel at ⊗ *	1	4			
Depth of false keel		5			
Length of the tread of the keel to the forefoot	128	0		Table of scantling, *Shipbuilder's Repository*	Measured from the aft side of keel
Location of the midship bend*	58.95		⁵⁄₁₂ length of gun deck (141.5ft)	Steel's *Vade Mecum*	Measured along the range of gun deck
Distance of forefoot to fore perpendicular (FP)	11	9	¹⁄₁₂ 141.5ft		
Length between perpendiculars (LBP)	139	9	Sum of 128ft + 11ft 9in		Distance of forefoot to FP plus tread of the keel
Siding of stem	1	3		Table of scantling, *Shipbuilder's Repository*	Measured at the gun deck. Used to find length of keel for tonnage
Breadth of beam	37	6		Table of scantling, *Shipbuilder's Repository*	Moulded breadth on table. Used as extreme breadth (Hackett).
Start of curve at the stem, and touch of the straight rabbet of the keel*	22	2	³⁄₅ beam (37ft)		Measured from aft of FP at the top of the keel using Hackett's moulded beam (37ft)
Length of keel for tonnage	118	0			Measured from aft side of sternpost, to touch forward
Registered tonnage	(850²²⁄₉₅ tons)			Carpenters' rule 1799	118 × 37 (keel × breadth) = 4336 × 18½ (half breadth) = 80771 ÷ 95 = 850²²⁄₉₅ registered tons.
Rake of the sternpost from aft perpendicular	2	11		Table, *Shipbuilder's Repository*	Measured at the height of the wing transom
Height of toptimber line	28	0	⅕ length gun deck (140ft)	Steel's *Vade Mecum*	Measured from the underside of the keel
Height of load waterline (LWL)	16	8	³⁄₅ height of top timbers		Measured from the top of the keel. Used to calculate displacement.
Height at ⊗ of port sill above LWL	5	3			Follows general rule; 5–6ft above load waterline in frigates
Depth in the hold	12	3	⁷⁄₂₁ moulded breadth (37ft)		Steel gives proportion ⁷⁄₂₀ measured from the upper side of beam of orlop to the strake next the limbers
Distance station X from FP	4	5		Table, *Shipbuilder's Repository*	This would have been the distance had Hackett carried his stations that far forward
In the fore body – distance ⊗ from FP	61	7		Tables, 'Bodies of a frigate of 36 guns', Steel's *Vade Mecum*	Total of fore and after bodies measured in feet = 120ft. The sum is used to calculate number of square and cant stations on the sheer plan
In the after body – station 7 from the aft perpendicular	58	5			
Area for square frames	120			Tables, 'Bodies of a frigate of 36 guns', Steel's *Vade Mecum*	The sum 120ft is subtracted from the LBP (139ft 9in) to obtain the number of feet for cants.
Area for cant timbers (running feet)	19	9			

* Appears as a notation on the Hackett draught
** A compendium of earlier works from Mungo Murray, 1765; *Shipbuilder's Repository*, 1789; William Sutherland, 1794; Hutchinson, 1787.

Hackett saw that these figures clearly allowed too little space for the cants. The table in the *Shipbuilder's Repository* indicates that the square frames should be placed between midships and station P forward and between midships and station 21 aft. Hackett felt, correctly, that 21 was too far forward so he fixed station 29 as the position of his last square frame aft. These timbers and those following aft to the after end of the quarterdeck are calculated as single frames with a siding of 12in in the first set of calculations:

After Body Frames

0 to 29 (64 single frames)	63ft 7in, rounded to 64ft 0in
29 to after end of quarterdeck	19ft 9in, rounded to 19ft 4in
Total	83ft 4in

These figures are carried over to the second set of calculations which include the frames forward of midships and the hawse timbers. Here Hackett has begun at the fore side of the midship station and carried his square frames as far forward as the theoretical joint line of frame bend N, then forward as far as the joint line for the theoretical frame bend X. This location appears as a faint pencil line on the draught.

Fore Body Frames

	ft	in
Single frames from the fore side of 0 to joint of N forward	33	
Single frames from joint line at N to joint line at X	19	9
Sub-total	52	9
(From after body calculation)		
Total, rounded	83	
plus hawse timbers	4	
Total for fore body frames	139	9

Note: Aft frame spaces are numbered on the fore side; fore frame spaces are lettered on the aft side.

Later Hackett would again alter the space for the square frames bends by increasing the number of cants in the after body, thus shifting their position to station 24. Positive evidence of this change comes from two sources. The first is a tick mark Hackett made on his scale above the 21ft line; when this mark is raised to the top of the keel it falls on what would be the after edge of the first cant frame bend number 24. The position of the fore and aft cants in the reconstructed lines plan is marked by a heavy dashed line representing their centres, and it is these centres which gives us our second proof. Hackett used these lines to position his cants on the body plan. The distance from the centreline on the half breadth at the waterlines and diagonals has been measured square to the centreline, indicating the angle each of these takes.

On the sheer Hackett also indicated the amount of room and space he planned to use at the midship mark above the keel. The frames would be sided 11in and the space 3.8in. To maintain these proportions he would have to reduce the number of spaces occupied by the square frames from fifty-four to forty-five and redistribute the additional nine spaces. To arrive at the solution found in the body plan, it would have been necessary to draw a framing diagram using 2.15ft for room and space. The erasures on the draught indicate that Hackett observed the convention for two timber supports under the port sills. They also confirm the shift of the timbers at the forecastle and quarter-deck. The following shows how he arrived at the room and space figure:

Final Room and Space Calculations

LBP 139ft 9in, less cants (43ft) = 96ft 9in
96ft 9in divided by 45 spaces for square frames = 2.15ft, or 25.8in, total room
  and space
25.8in less siding of frame bend (22in) = 3.8in room

The next notation made on the keel by Hackett marks the location of the joint for the boxing of the stem. It is shown as a vertical dotted line just forward of station O. Following this mark, running up the stem, are the numbers 1–5. These correspond to the waterlines, with the exception of number 5 which represents the point on the stem where the upper height of breadth would terminate at the fore perpendicular on the sheer and half-breadth elevations. Hackett has also used this point on the half breadth for the termination of the dotted toptimber line at the bow.

The first waterline above the keel on the sheer is positioned at the height of the deadrise, 4 is the load waterline line and the two between, are placed at the designer's discretion.

Perhaps most puzzling of all the lines on the sheer elevation are the curved lines above the keel. They are drawn nearly parallel to one another, and the first has its height set at the deadrise at midships. This curve and the two above match the diagonal lines on the body plan at midships, but beyond this point they do not. If the diagonals of the forebody were projected to the sheer they would take on the shape shown on the reconstructed lines of the sheer. It is possible that the diagonals shown on the body plan may have been intended to represent diagonals for harpin moulds. The curves as drawn on Hackett's sheer appear to be the locations for the futtock heads. A slight adjustment of a few inches in the middle one brings the curve in line with the lower futtock. The heads of the third futtocks fall in line with the lower height of breadth for most of its length up to about station P. The heads of the futtocks then stay approximately in line with the middle of the main wale.

The lower height of breadth line appears on all the elevations, but on the

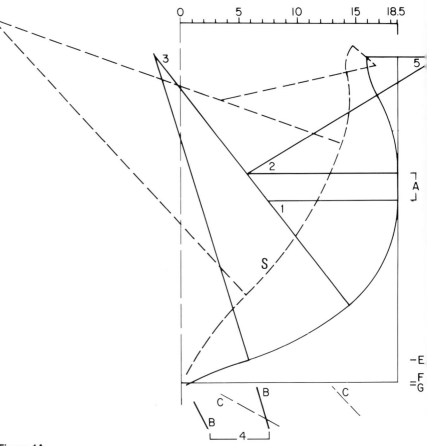

Figure 1A

Midship bend ————	
S cant bend – – – – –	
1	Lower breadth sweep
2	Upper breadth sweep
3	Reconciling sweep
4	Deadrise sweep
5	Toptimber sweep
A	Dead flat
B	Segment of deadrise sweep
C	Segment of S cant floor sweep
D	Toptimber line
E	Limit of deadrise
F	Base line
G	Middle of rabbet of the keel

main body plan is shown only as a short diagonal up to station S in the forebody and to station 30 aft. Beyond station 30 Hackett made corrections, as can be seen from the erasures made at 30 and 33, and at S.

The upper height of breadth line, normally now shown on any elevation, does appear in the reconstructed lines and framing diagram as a reference point for the reader. It was used in conjunction with the existing station curves for stations S and 27–33 to reconstruct the body plan.

In the reconstruction of Hackett's arcs, we can show how the curves are extended above the short diagonal line for the toptimbers in the fore and after

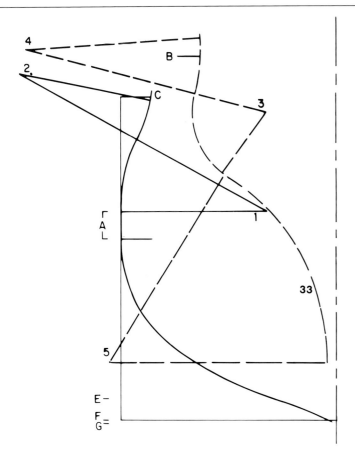

Figure 1B

Midship bend ─────────
Frame bend 33 ─ ─ ─ ─ ─
1	Upper breadth sweep
2	Toptimber sweep
3	Upper breadth sweep
4	Toptimber sweep
5	Floor sweep
A	Dead flat
B	Toptimber – bend 30
C	Toptimber line
E	Limit of deadrise
F	Base line
G	Middle of rabbet of keel

bodies. These short diagonals, however, define the limits of those timbers in the waist only. If projected to the sheer they define the underside of the deck at the sides for the quarterdeck and forecastle. Hackett has drawn in the toptimber lines for these areas on his body plan above the diagonals, which also stop at station S in the forebody and 33 aft; these features are shown in Figures 1A and 1B. With the end of this diagonal and the horizontal line representing the upper edge of the wing transom, Hackett gives us the upper limits of the fore side of his fashion timber.

We noted above the increase in the number of cants in the fore and after

bodies, and the measurement for the room and space: both these influenced the *shift of timbers* seen in the disposition of the frames. As a consequence, Hackett's original number and letter system was altered. We can see from the reconstructed lines on the sheer that station 33, when compared with the framing diagram, falls on the fore side of the fashion timber 34. The cants 24 and 27 are also measured on the fore side. What is interesting is that station 30 on Hackett's original draught has been measured as a square frame at right angles to the centreline of the body and the half-breadth, measuring along the waterlines, and that it appears as the last designated frame space on his sheer elevation. The centre of the cant bend number 30 is used as an example in the reconstructed frames to illustrate the minor difference between Hackett's shape of number 30 cant and the canted version shown in the reconstructed lines elevation.

In the forebody Hackett used an entirely different method to describe the S cant. Again he used the fore edge of the cant drawn in the reconstruction but this time he measured the distance to the diagonals square from the centreline of the half-breadth, then transferred those distances to the corresponding diagonals in the body plan, with the one exception of the first diagonal. He then transferred the distance of the first diagonal on the half-breadth to the horizontal width of the floor. At the upper edge of the S cant he has indicated the flare taken by rail and the top of the timberhead.

A final interesting feature of Hackett's draught is the placement of the decks. It appears that he used the information already obtained for the location of the underside of the decks at midships, and then once again referred to the tables in Steel's *Vade Mecum* and the *Repository*. The depth in the hold gives the height of the berth deck. The distance between it and the gun deck above is 5ft 10in. The *Repository* calls for 1in more, as is true for the height to the quarterdeck, fore and aft. The height in the waist is the same as Hackett's measure of 6ft 0in. These internal measurements are taken from the 32-gun frigate in the *Repository* while those for the structure of the hull have been taken from a 38-gun frigate. Hackett deviated from the 4½in round-up of the gundeck listed in Steel and the *Repository* and kept his to 3½in. The height of the light room, filling room and magazine reveals the height of the platforms aft as 6ft 0in, and also confirms the cable tier as 5ft 0in. The last source for William Hackett's siding of the midship bend comes from the table of scantling in the 1765 edition of Mungo Murray. This table is based on the breadth of the vessel, and it appears that Hackett used the measurements for a vessel 36ft broad.

The terms berth deck and gun deck are those used at the period. They are used here to be consistent with Hackett's notes, and the Fox and *Essex* papers.

CONSTRUCTION, REBUILDS AND COLOUR SCHEME

Changes in the gun deck forward of midships, made shortly after the *Essex* was launched on 30 September 1799, do not appear on the draught; they were necessitated by the installation of the Brodie stove in the galley under the forecastle. The stove and the armourer's forge had both been imported from England, originally for use on the frigate *Boston*. Joseph Waters arranged with the *Boston* Committee for the stove to be sent to Salem where it was stored, partially dismantled, in a warehouse. The *Boston* was a smaller frigate than the *Essex* and it is possible that it was too large for the intended vessel, although no reason was given for its rejection by the committee. When time came to install the stove, it was found to be too large for the *Essex* as well. This required moving the fore riding bitts, and altering the position of the scuttle just forward of the bitts at the gun deck and the decks above and below. This alteration, and the changes ordered by Captain Preble after his arrival, added

42 days to the building time. Among the changes made by Captain Preble were the replacement of the wooden stanchions in the railings in the tops, the railing along the gangboards, and the hammock cranes at the rails.

The *Essex* seems to have retained her good sailing qualities as late as December 1805, when Commodore Preble's memorandum prepared for President Thomas Jefferson on the condition of the frigates of the United States, stated: '*Essex* — A prime sailer, and the best model of a Frigate (of her rate) in the Navy — requires rebuilding from the wales up.' These recommendations were not carried out until the *Essex* went into ordinary in 1807.

A preliminary survey made by Josiah Fox in 1807 indicated that seventy-five of her lower futtocks would need replacement; ultimately more than ninety were replaced. These repairs were to be carried out while the vessel was afloat, and Fox expressed his concerns about this method in a letter to Secretary of the Navy Robert Smith in June 1807. Fox identified a number of dangers which he felt might arise from the methods employed for the repairs:

> The principal dangers might arise from graving pieces secured in the planks to be removed; loosening of the butts; defective places in the planks; and also from removing too many planks at a time thereby leaving the planks without sufficient security, which may occasion the ship to strain when heaving down.

The sag in the quarterdeck, also mentioned in the first survey, was due, Fox felt, to the lack of pillars in the cabin below. Although there is no mention of pillars being installed it is likely that they were fitted during the 1807–9 refit.

While work was still in progress in January 1808, Fox suggested reducing the housing 9in a side, and shifting the position of the gunports so as to clear the shrouds. In his final report on 5 June 1809, he tells us that these changes were made in addition to raising her topsides, wales and thick strakes, settling the lower deck 2in, shortening the rake of the counter and cutting a row of air ports fore and aft. At this time the size of the gunports was also altered, in preparation for the change in the armament of the *Essex*. This is confirmed by a letter from Captain Charles Stewart to Secretary of the Navy Robert Smith dated 10 February 1809, requesting seven additional 32pdr carronades and eighteen carronnade carriages and slides proposed for the quarterdeck and forecastle. The number of ports was increased from ten (1808) to fourteen on the quarterdeck in February 1809. There was also a change in the dimensions of the magazine made during the refit but not mentioned in the final report by Fox.

After the refit by Fox was completed in 1809, the reputation of the *Essex* as a fine sailer was, for a time, lost. Changes to her hull form are suggested by the alterations made to her topsides. Later, Master Commandant David Porter was to complain of the disproportion of her masts and spars. It is not clear whether Porter was referring to the yards alone or to the whole spar plan in relation to the hull.

It is likely that Donald McIntire of Salem designed and executed all the carved work for the frigate *Essex*. Although there is no information to confirm this assumption, a painting at the Peabody Museum at Salem, thought to represent the *Essex*, gives a broadside view of the vessel illustrating an American Indian as the figurehead. Other examples of McIntire's work would suggest that the trailboards depicted in the Peabody painting are his design, and as McIntire was a trained architect as well as a ship carver with a strong classical influence, it could be expected that his figurehead would also reflect this influence. Since no drawings have been found of the figurehead, the cat's face at the end of the cathead, or the work at the stern and quarter gallery, it is

ultimately impossible to say if these elements in the painting truly represent the work of McIntire, or whether these are the artist's additions.

The style used by the artist to represent the hull raises a number of questions. Among them are the designs on the quarter gallery, which may have been carved or painted. His use of white paint to depict the curve of the gallery below the windows might be the method of choice of an unskilled hand, yet it leads me to believe that what appears as lattice work on the hollow top might also be highlights illustrating the curved edge of shingles. This idea might also apply to the designs on the upper and lower finishings of the quarter gallery, but more questionable is the eagle with outstretched wings across the face of the drop. It seems an unlikely design, given the recessed extreme curves of this area and for this reason I have omitted it from the drawings. It is generally accepted that the colours in the painting do represent the paint work for the *Essex*.

The colours depicted match those listed in the account recorded by William Luscomb, painter and glazier, who worked on the hull and spars of the *Essex*. She is shown with a black hull above the copper with a broad ochre stripe running the length of the hull. A pale yellow is carried to the headrails and cathead, and the inboard face of the bridle port lid. During the first cruise of the *Essex*, Captain Preble had the interior of the gun deck painted yellow, perhaps to lighten an otherwise dark interior. The remaining port lids have their inboard faces painted vermilion red. A warm orange ochre is used as a background colour for the vine and flower design of the trailboards. The green vine is punctuated with small vermilion red flowers. The Indian figurehead wears a white cape with a wide green border; the girdle is spotted with red and green, perhaps representing coloured feathers, and the hair is black topped with feathers. Inboard, the knightheads and lower portions of the masts are vermilion red. The mast doublings and spars are black, but the outer end of the jibboom, flying jibboom, boomkins and masts, up to and above the caps, are all natural unpainted wood. It is also possible that the ochre stripe on the hull represents the natural wood payed over with tar. The boat at the stern is painted white with a blue stripe in the middle of a broader black one.

Construction of the *Essex* was assigned to Enos Briggs, a longtime resident and shipbuilder at Salem. It was he who placed the advertisement in the *Salem Gazette* on 23 November, calling for white oak timber for the hull, and more especially the keel, which was to be 16in square, in four lengths, totalling 146ft. By the end of December Enos Briggs had obtained the timber for the Salem frigate, but it would be several more months before the keel was laid. How much time was spent by William Hackett working on the lines from the end of October until the end of November can only be guessed. Yet enough must have been done so that Enos Briggs could contract with the Salem committee to construct a ship of 850 tons at $30.00 a ton on 30 November 1798. The schedule of Hackett's movements from the time the *Essex* was authorized to be built in early October 1798 until he took his final leave of Salem in November 1799 is recorded in Table 3.

While it is thought that the hull, outboard planking and much of the inboard works were constructed with white oak, considerable use was also made of pine. It was believed the chemical interaction of these two materials was responsible for much of the rot of the frames. In a letter to Captain Edward Preble dated 8 April 1803, the Secretary of the Navy calls attention to this problem with the *Essex*: 'It has been found by experience that the filling in a ship with pine timber is injurious to the frame. The frigate *Essex* is an instance of this.' It is not clear if this concern was recognized during the Fox refit of 1807–9, since his estimate for timber required for the interior of the hull does

1798

October	9	Letter to Benjamin Goodhue from Secretary of the Navy Benjamin Stoddard authorizing work to begin on the frigate *Essex*
	24	Letter to William Hackett from William Gray of the Salem Frigate Committee asking him to come to Salem to discuss the frigate
	30	Hackett put on the payroll. Assumed to be in Salem at that time
November	6	Hackett and Ichabod Nichols go to Boston to confer with the Boston Frigate Committee
	7	Hackett and Nichols return to Salem
	8	Hackett returns to Salisbury
	13	Nichols goes to Salisbury to bring Hackett back to Salem
	23	Enos Briggs' advertisement appears in the *Salem Gazette* (146ft keel, 16in square, 4 pieces)
	23–30	Enos Briggs contracts with the Salem Committee to construct a ship of 850 tons at $30.00 per ton (including the timber) Hackett returns to Salisbury at or before the end of November
December	1	Hackett at Salisbury

1799

January	11	Hackett at Salisbury; paid $100 on account
	11–30	Hackett returns to Salem. Remains until 30 January
	30	Hackett returns to Salisbury
February	–	Hackett at Salem for 12 days (exact dates not known)
March	11	Briggs starts work on the keel. Requests that Hackett come to approve the scarfs
March	11–	Briggs spends 25½ days lofting moulds
April	2	
April	2–	Hackett returns to Salem. Twenty days at Webb Inn in April, remaining time lodged with
November	30	Jonathan Brown
April	13	Keel is laid
	23	Floor timbers installed on the keel
May	28	Hackett writes to his son requesting his 'sweeps' to draw the final draught of the *Essex*
September	30	*Essex* launched
November	30	Hackett returns to Salisbury

Subscription Funds	Dollars	Cents
Constructor	921	54
Building	26,616	64
Iron work	8371	94
Cordage	10,075	03
Sundries (spars, boars, blocks)	12,723	91
Painting and plumbing	2256	35
Carving	410	00
Duck	3731	74
Anchors	1081	92
Copper bolts	4339	05
Sailmakers (labour)	730	24
Tradesmen (labour)	2735	36
Commissions on 73,993.72 @ 2% (Navy agent Joseph Waters)	1479	87
	75,473.	59

Government funds	Dollars	Cents
Ordnance, military stores, kentlage, copper	31,992	76
Ship's stores (12 months)	12,709	19
Provisions (12 months)	12,304	52
Slop clothing	3868	79
Hospital stores	1526	20
Extra – sail, duck, anchors, spars, cables, (labour and commissions)	16,812	72
	154,687.	77

Nearly half the cost of building the *Essex* was born by the subscription funds, thus making her eligible as a loan to the government. The actual cost to subscribers before the commission fee of Joseph Waters was $73,993.72 which left a deficit of $773.59 over the subscribed amount of $74,700.00.

not square with the type used. Some shipbuilders at this period used rock salt, as they do today, packed between the frames in the hold to minimize the effect of moisture, but there is no evidence that this was done with the *Essex*.

Because we have only fragmentary accounts from contracts with other builders of the period we can only assume that some of the methods used at other yards were adopted by either Hackett or Briggs. Both men, especially Hackett, were experienced and were familiar with other builders. Hackett's detailed notes would indicate that he was observant and interested in the methods of others. It is quite possible that he incorporated the method of dovetailing the beams into the clamps of the gun bearing decks to minimize the racking of the deck from the discharge of the guns. The exposed edges of the overhead beam might also have been chamfered to lessen the possibility of splinters flying off during combat.

American shipbuilders seemed to favour the use of planking with fair edges in parallel lengths rather than the use of top- or hook-and-butt planking used by their English cousins, and this is confirmed by Hackett's notes, so it is assumed in the reconstruction of the hull planking that parallel lengths were used. Thrift might have been a factor in the use of stiff brown paper as doubling for the coppered bottom rather than felt, or it may simply have been used to minimize the puckering associated with the use of felt. After the ship had been hoved down to complete the coppering, her false keel, previously coppered, was then installed. Good sense did not override thrift in the use of wood for stanchions in the waist, hammock cranes or railings in the tops. Splinters from these during battle could be lethal, so Captain Preble had them replaced with iron before the *Essex* left on her first cruise.

ARMAMENT AND FLAGS

During the period 1790–98 there was no Navy Department and naval affairs were under the jurisdiction of the War Department. In September in 1796, preparations were being made to procure ordnance for the *Essex*, among the three frigates then under construction. A letter dated 13 September 1796 from the Secretary of War to the Secretary of the Treasury details the conditions to be adhered to in contracts for the manufacture of cannons that would be issued by the Treasury Department. Two of the conditions set forth are of interest because they illustrate the point that American guns of that period were intended to be patterned after English designs.

The first example is condition number two, 'That the twenty four nine pounders and twelve six pounders conform exactly in weight, bore, caliber, and length, to British Ship Guns of the same dimensions now in use.' The second example, number seven, is particularly relevant to the guns carried by the *Essex*:

That the trunnions must be perpendicular to the vertical plan which is supposed to pass through the touch hole, and to cut the bore into two equal parts. That the *upper part of the trunnion shall be level with the center of the caliber, or bore* [author's italics], and that the usual relative weight be preserved between the breech and the chase.

Although rated as a 32-gun frigate, the *Essex* carried twenty-six 12pdrs on her gun deck and ten 6pdrs on the quarterdeck, two of which would be used at the forecastle as needed. All her guns were of English manufacture and were acquired from two sources — the Navy agent in Boston and the Boston Frigate Committee.

In a letter to the Navy agent, Joseph Waters, Secretary of the Navy Stoddart gives the lengths of the long 12pdrs and 6pdrs at 7½ft and 5½ft respectively. These were to be supplied by Lane & Salter or Foxall & Co, while those offered by the Boston Frigate Committee would be those left over from a parcel of guns purchased at Halifax. This set of guns would be shorter by 6in and from 3cwt to 4cwt lighter. The Committee's guns were all 12pdrs weighing between 23cwt and 25cwt.

Nothing is mentioned about the position of the trunnions, but because all were of English origin, it can be assumed that the trunnion centreline was below that of the bore. This could explain the difficulties encountered by Captain Preble when the time came to mount the guns on their carriages. When he inspected them in November 1799 he found all of them too high for the port openings. He had the guns dismounted and the carriages sent ashore to be altered.

A drawing of the gun carriages of the *Essex* is among the Fox papers at the Peabody Museum at Salem. On the drawing is a notation which reads, 'beds and skids for spar deck not begun'. The drawing is not dated, but the date implied by the notation is during the 1807–9 refit when the *Esses*'s ports were altered for the carronades.

An abstract from the journal of Captain Edward Preble dated Friday 14 February 1800 reads, 'Dismounted two of the quarter-deck guns and stored them below, as they could not be worked clear of the main shrouds.' This statement appears to confirm the position of the shrouds during the first cruise to the Mediterranean as that indicated on William Hackett's draught. The second foremost leg of the main shrouds obstructs the first gunport aft of the break of the quarterdeck, rendering guns at that position useless. Hackett had called for six ports a side on the quarterdeck on his draught. However, it is possible that this port was boarded over during December of that year when the *Essex* put in for repairs at New York. Her main lower mast was replaced, and a new gang of shrouds was installed at that time. If the port had been boarded over during the repairs it would explain the five ports on the Peabody painting, and the total of ten ports on the quarterdeck found in the Fox survey of 1808, prior to repairs. After that, in February 1809, the *Essex* is listed as carrying seven ports a side. Later, in January 1810, her armament would again change to 32pdr carronades on the gun deck, in place of her long guns.

Included in the Gunner's indent are the small arms furnished by the Navy Department through the firm of Foxall & Salter, who also provided a set of signal colours. The small arms listed were: 100 cutlasses, 60 muskets and bayonets, 30 pairs of pistols and 100 boarding pikes.

The Armourer's indent lists a forge. A description of the forge and its equipment are among the *Essex* papers at the Peabody museum at Salem, and it also appears in the appendices of Philip C F Smith's book *The Frigate Essex Papers*. The forge shown in the drawings is theoretical and was drawn after a discussion with a master gunsmith familiar with forges of that period. He felt the beehive shape would be the most efficient one for generating heat quickly for the purpose of heating shot to be used as 'hot shot'. The tray under the forge held the shot to fill the furnace, then when hot it was removed with the ring shovel. Prior to loading, the gun was packed with a wad of wet straw and another of clay to prevent premature firing of the gun. The forge would be positioned about amidships on the gun deck and is estimated to be approximately three to four feet square.

Prior to the return home of the *Essex* from Batavia in June 1800, Captain Preble issued a set of signal colours to the fifteen vessels the *Essex* would escort. The last vessel listed in the table, the ship *Magnus*, appears not to be among that returning group. The signal flags would make 108 days signals, and were

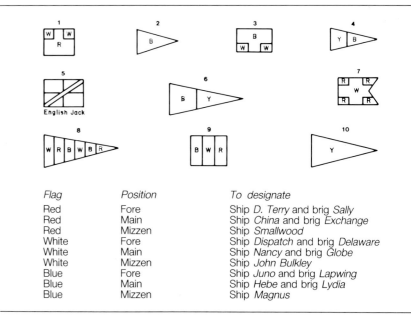

Flag	Position	To designate
Red	Fore	Ship *D. Terry* and brig *Sally*
Red	Main	Ship *China* and brig *Exchange*
Red	Mizzen	Ship *Smallwood*
White	Fore	Ship *Dispatch* and brig *Delaware*
White	Main	Ship *Nancy* and brig *Globe*
White	Mizzen	Ship *John Bulkley*
Blue	Fore	Ship *Juno* and brig *Lapwing*
Blue	Main	Ship *Hebe* and brig *Lydia*
Blue	Mizzen	Ship *Magnus*

issued to each vessel in the convoy, along with a code for night signals, on 14 June 1800; these are shown above.

Not until the official regulation of 1795 was any attempt made to establish a design for the national ensign. Naval flags were also effected at that date. While the regulation specified fifteen alternating red and white stripes with fifteen white stars on a blue field next to the hoist, this last part of the regulation produced a number of variations based largely on the whim of the flag makers. Among the more popular variants was the design shown in the drawings. This flag was normally flown at the peak, but would be carried at each masthead during battle. The jack was an adaptation of the blue field with white stars; it was also flown at the fore mast. The commissioning pennant would have been carried at the main truck when the *Essex* left Salem on her first cruise. The design for this was also subject to alteration in the arrangement of the stars, but it is shown in the drawings as illustrated in the Peabody Museum's painting of the *Essex*. This pennant would be replaced by the Commodore's broad pennant, designating the vessel as the flagship of the squadron. The blue swallow-tailed flag carried fifteen white stars in a circle representing each of the states in the republic, and one large central one, representing the nation.

RIGGING AND SAILS
On 20 February 1799 a contract for spars was signed between the Salem Frigate Committee and Nathaniel Guptail of Portsmouth, New Hampshire. He agreed to supply two of each spar required with the exception of the lower masts, driver boom, crossjack, and spritsail yards. Of these there would be only one. The lower masts, bowsprit, main and fore yards would all be pine and the remainder of spruce. This contract did not furnish all of the spars for the *Essex* nor those needed for the ship's boats. These were provided by Hawkes and Babbidge of Salem. The studdingsail yards, flying jib and mizzen boom are missing from Guptail's list, as is the dolphin striker. This last spar appears in a list of the *Essex* spars at about 1808 during the period of her last refit. At that same time skyscraper masts were added to all three masts, and royal studdingsail booms and yards added to the main and fore. The ringtail

TABLE 5: **ARMAMENT CHANGES AND RELATED ORDERS**

1799

December	Hackett's design, *Essex*: 44 ports – 12 quarterdeck, 4 forecastle, 28 gun deck (including 2 bridle ports)

1800

14 February	Preble dismounted 2 quarterdeck guns in the wake of the shrouds – stored below
25 December	*Put into New York for repairs. New Main lower mast and shrouds installed

1808

	First Fox survey: 10 ports total on quarterdeck, 26 on gun deck (excluding 2 bridle ports)
20 January	*Captain Thomas Tingey, Commandant Washington Navy Yard to Secretary of Navy Robert Smith* Suggests making immediate change in armament on *Essex* since topsides now being replaced. Change in position of shrouds also needed

1809

6 February	*Robert Smith to Captain Charles Stewart* You will assume command of the *Essex*, superintend equipment, prepare her for service
February	*Second Fox survey*: 46 ports total – 14 ports on quarterdeck, 4 forecastle, 26 gun deck (excluding 2 bridle ports)
10 February	*Captain Stewart to Robert Smith* List of required crew for 46-gun frigate *Essex*
10 February	*Captain Stewart to Robert Smith* Requests 7 additional 32pdr carronades, also 18 carriages and slides proposed for the quarterdeck and forecastle
31 March	*Acting Secretary of the Navy Charles W Goldsborough to Captain John Smith* You will assume command of the *Essex*
March	*Essex on Station at Hampton Roads*
2 June	*Thomas Tingey to Secretary of the Navy Paul Hamilton* Work progress slow on fitting carronade carriages at Washington Navy Yard. Requests permission to send *Essex* to Norfolk to complete the work as suggested by Captain William Bainbridge

1810

21 January	*Captain John Smith to Paul Hamilton* Acknowledges agreement of Hamilton to more efficient armament for the *Essex*. Requests order for 24 carronade carriages and slides. Tells of previous difficulties with installation of quarterdeck carriages, thereby requests *execution attained* in vicinity (Norfolk) where she can remain until work is completed (gun deck)
6 February	*Paul Hamilton to Captain John Smith* 32pdr carronades being cast at Foxall & Co
10 February	*Captain Smith to Paul Hamilton* Receiving order for making 24 carronade carriages at Norfolk. Will proceed immediately. Suggests lowering for end of orlop deck. Request denied by Hamilton

Guns

1799 December	36 guns total: ten long 6pdrs for the quarterdeck and forecastle, twenty-six long 12pdrs for gun deck
1809 February	46 guns total: eighteen 32pdr carronades for the quarterdeck and forecastle (plus two long 12pdr chase guns), twenty-six long 12pdrs on gun deck
1811 August	46 guns total: sixteen 32 pdr carronades, three long 12pdrs on spar deck; twenty-four 32pdr carronades, three long 12pdrs on gun deck until capture

* Possible boarding up of the first port.

TABLE 6: **MAST AND SPAR DIMENSIONS**

Masts	Length		Diam	Head		Pole	
	ft	in	in	ft	in	ft	in
Main	85		27	13		–	
Main topmast	55		18½	7½		–	
Main topgallant	43		12			15	0
Fore	79		26	12	8	–	
Fore topmast	46	2½	15⅞	6	8¾	–	
Fore topgallant	23	1½	9			14	0
Mizzen	75		21	10		–	
Mizzen topmast	40		14	5	6½	–	
Mizzen topgallant	34		9½			12	0
Bowsprit*	54		26	36			
Jibboom	39	3½	14	26	2		
Flying jibboom	43	8	7⅞	17	5		

Spars	Length		Diam	Arm	
	ft	in	in	ft	in
Main yard	80	0	20	4	10
Main topsail yard	58	0	14½	3	6
Main topgallant yard	40	0	10	2	2
Main royal yard	30	0	7		12½
Main lower studdingsail boom	40	10	10		
Main lower studdingsail swing boom	44	6	8½		
Main topmast studdingsail boom	30	7½	7		
Main topgallant studdingsail boom	27	6¾	6		
Main lower studdingsail yard	22	9	4½		
Main topmast studdingsail yard	17	0	3½		
Main topgallant studdingsail yard	15	6	3		
Fore yard	77		19	2	10¾
Fore topsail yard	54		13½	4	1
Fore topgallant yard	37		9½	1	10
Fore royal yard	30		7		10¼
Fore lower studdingsail boom	40		10		
Fore lower studdingsail swing boom	39		8½		
Fore topmast studdingsail boom	30		7		
Fore topgallant studdingsail boom	27		6		
Fore lower studdingsail yard	22	8	4½		
Fore topmast studdingsail yard	21	0	4		
Fore topgallant studdingsail yard	15	6	3		
Crossjack yard	54		14	4	10
Mizzen topsail yard	42		10½	2	1½
Mizzen topgallant yard	30		7½	1	4
Mizzen royal yard	20		5		6½
Spritsail yard	54		13½		5¾
Spritsail topsail yard	35		10		4½
Driver	57		14		
Mizzen gaff	46		11		
Dolphin striker (below cap)**	13	1	6½		
Ensign staff**	32		7½		
Jack staff**	16		4¾		

* Length inboard from the fore side of the stem to the aft side of the bitts 16ft. Length above includes 12in heel.
** Not on the Guptail list. Dimensions taken from the Fox 1809 and Navy yard 1808 lists.

boom and yard mentioned in the rigging contract with McClennan & Saunders only appears on the 1808 list.

The various spar lists found in the appendices to Philip C F Smith's book *The Frigate Essex Papers* give a detailed account of these differences. Included is the handwritten list made by Enos Briggs of Guptail's original proposed dimensions. This same list found its way into Captain Preble's papers, presumably passed on in the event of needed repairs. For reconstruction purposes the dimensions for the flying jibboom and dolphin striker have been taken from the 1808 list, and the remaining spars' dimensions from the Guptail list which accompanied the contract.

The man responsible for converting the raw sticks into the spars was Luke Laighton of Portsmouth. His correspondence with Joseph Waters confirms the use of iron hoops on the bowsprit, and, presumably, the masts in conjunction with the woolding. At the end of January, during the first cruise of the *Essex*, she sprung her mainmast in a gale, some three feet above the wedges between decks. The following day the crew was set to fishing and woolding the mast and getting up the preventer shrouds. Preble's letter to the Secretary of the Navy reporting the damage to the masts and rigging describes the iron work on the masts as being of very poor quality. During that storm, the fore and main trestletrees gave way, as did the rigging and most of the ironwork. At the end of December the mainmast was removed and a new one put in its place ten days later. Her mainmast and foremast would be altered during the 1807–9 refit, after which the *Essex* lost her fine sailing qualities. When Porter took

TABLE 7: RIGGING AND SAILS

Quantity Fathoms	Size (circum) in	Use	Weight cwt–qtr–lb
140	8½	Lower shrouds	18–0–0
22	13	Main stay	8–2–7
22	9½	Spring stay	4–1–18
80	5½	Main top shrouds	4–3–7
120	6¼	Main top backstays	10–3–14
60	3¼	Main topgallant shrouds	2–0–11
80	3¾	Main topgallant backstays	1–2–16
60	6	Main topsail sheets	2–3–0
40	6¼	Main topstay, hawser laid	3–2–10
40	5½	Main topstay springstay, hawser laid	4–3–5
–	–	–	4–3–16*
60	6	Topsail tyes	4–3–21
60	6	Breechings (gunner)	5–0–0
		3 coils 3¼in	3–1–2
		4 coils of 3in	1–2–6
		6 coils of spunyarn 6 yarns	1–3–21
		5 coils of spunyarn 4 yarns	
		1 coil of spunyarn 2 yarns	
		1 coil of spunyarn 3 yarns	
		1 coil of 60 fathoms 5¾in four-strand	

Cables
5 16in cables (32,661lbs)
1 stream cable
1 hawser
1 towline (3526lbs)
1 messenger (1565lbs)

Sails manufactured by Buffum & Howard

Square

2	Spritsail topsail	2	Main royal sail
2	Spritsail course	2	Main topgallant sail
2	Fore royal sail	2	Main topsail
2	Fore topgallant sail	2	Main course
2	Fore topsail	4	Main topgallant studdingsails
2	Fore course	4	Main topmast studdingsails
4	Fore topgallant studdingsails	4	Main lower studdingsails
4	Fore topmast studdingsails	2	Mizzen topgallant sail
4	Fore lower studdingsails	2	Mizzen topsail
		2	Royal sail

Fore & aft

2	Flying jib	2	Mizzen topgallant staysail
2	Jib	2	Mizzen topsail staysail
2	Fore topmast staysail	2	Boom driver
2	Fore staysail	2	Mizzen driver
2	Main topgallant staysail	2	Storm staysail
2	Main topmast staysail		
2	Main middle staysail		

* Indicates missing item from Hackett's list of rigging cordage.

command he complained bitterly of the disproportion of her masts and yards, and suggested replacing the foremast with the reworked mainmast, and then building a new main. These new dimensions are listed as Item 566 in the Fox papers at the Peabody Museum.

The *Essex* carried a total of thirteen square sails (including spritsail course and topsail), a driver, twelve steering sails (studdingsails) and eleven staysails. These were provided by Buffum & Howard of Salem who also provided the ship's boats' sails and canvas covers.

The *Essex* carried at least one lightning rod, probably on her mainmast truck. Both the rod and conductor chain were made by Paul Revere. The copper rod was silvered and it is assumed the fine chain was wrought of copper.

Possibly the rod was fixed French fashion through a system of plates and connecting chains beginning at the highest point at the truck of the main royal pole mast to the topgallant mast cap, then down to the lower caps, and along the aftermost leg of the main shroud to the channels. Here the chain was flaked for instant release at the first sign of storm, when it could be dropped over the side. Three or four fathoms was considered sufficient length to assure that the chain would remain immersed during a storm. Whether it had more than one leg, as the French used, is not known.

A document from the US Navy Board's New Book dated 6 October 1796 illustrates plan views of tops for a First Class frigate and for a sloop of war. The design of the tops represents a radical departure from those used on English ships of war at that period. Because they are nearer in size, the proportions of the tops for the sloop of war were used in the reconstruction of the tops for the *Essex*. The length of the crosstrees had to be altered from the proportions given in Steel's tables to suit the shape of the tops, the foremost one shorter, while the aftermost crosstree was increased in length. The main top was the basis for the remaining two. No provision was indicated on the drawings for the crowsfeet called for in Steel's rigging lists, and which appear in the painting of the *Essex*. These have been added to the tops on the strength of the painting, the usual practice of the period and Steel's list. Two sleepers, or upper crosstrees, span the tops at the fore and after edges of the lubber's hole. At the centre forward of the foremost sleeper is a small oval hole for the lower yard slings. Behind it and on top of the sleeper is a half-round bolster.

SERVICE HISTORY
Captain Edward Preble was not the first choice of the frigate committee as commander of the *Essex*, but it is fortunate that he became so, in light of her difficult passage to Newport and around the Cape of Good Hope to Batavia. A man of lesser mettle might not have performed as well in response to the damage inflicted on the *Essex* and her crew by the violent storms she encountered.

One of the last acts of the Adams administration was to order a squadron, under Commodore Richard Dale, back to the Mediterranean to protect American shipping from the Barbary pirates. The *Essex*, now under the command of Captain William Bainbridge, sailed with the frigates *President* and *Philadelphia* and the schooner *Enterprise*.

With the Jefferson administration about to take over the reins of government, Benjamin Stoddart made an attempt to preserve the Navy as it had grown during the Federalist period. However, the Jeffersonians and the anti-navalists in the Congress passed the Peace Establishment Act on 3 March 1801, the day before Jefferson was inaugurated. As a result of this act, some twenty smaller Navy ships were sold and seven frigates, including the *Essex*, were placed in ordinary (reserve). Only six frigates were to remain on active service. By June of that year the Pasha of Tripoli had declared war on the United States for non-payment of tribute, but not until the following February did Congress recognize a state of war with Tripoli. The Barbary Wars would continue until June 1805, and a permanent peace would not be established until after the War of 1812 when Commodore Stephen Decatur effected a peacy treaty with the Dey of Algiers in May of 1815.

The Treaty of Paris ended the war with France in December of 1801. In spite of the position of neutrality taken by the United States in the European war, her shipping would continue to be interrupted by the warring nations.

The *Essex* was brought out of ordinary in the spring of 1804 and again sailed to the Mediterranean with Captain James Barron, under Commodore Samuel

TABLE 8: **BELAYING**

No	Item	Side	Belaying location	No	Item	Side	Belaying location
Crossjack				*Flying jib*			
1.	Truss pendent	P	Cleat on mast	54.	Stay	–	Spritsail collar
2.	Nave line	—	Cleat on mast	55.	Halliard	S	Breasthook pin rail
3.	Braces	P&S	Main pin rail	56.	Downhauler–inhauler (for traveller)	P	Breasthook pin rail
4.	Lifts	P&S	Mizzen pin rail	57.	Sheets	P&S	Timberhead at forecastle
				58.	Tacks	P&S	Made fast round jibboom
Mizzen topsail							
5.	Lifts	P&S	Mizzen pin rail	*Spritsail*			
6.	Halliard	P	Cleat on bulwark	59.	Braces	P&S	Deck cleat at forecastle
7.	Braces	P&S	Mizzen topsail sheet bitts	60.	Lifts	P&S	Breasthook pin rail
8.	Clew lines	P&S	Mizzen pin rail	61.	Bunt lines	P&S	Breasthook pin rail
9.	Reef tackles	P&S	Mizzen pin rail	62.	Clue lines	P&S	Breasthook pin rail
10.	Bunt lines	P&S	Mizzen pin rail	63.	Sheets	P&S	Knighthead
11.	Bowlines	P&S	Middle pin rail				
12.	Sheets	P&S	Mizzen topsail sheet bitts	*Spritsail topsail*			
				64.	Braces	P&S	Deck cleat at forecastle
Mizzen topgallant sail				65.	Lifts	P&S	Breasthook pin rail
13.	Lifts	P&S	Mizzen lower top	66.	Bunt lines	P&S	Breasthook pin rail
14.	Halliards	P	Mizzen lower top	67.	Clew lines	P&S	Breasthook pin rail
15.	Braces	P	Main lower top (first deadeye)	68.	Sheets	P&S	Knighthood
16.	Clew lines	P&S	Mizzen lower top				
17.	Bowlines	P&S	Mizzen lower top	*Main course*			
18.	Sheets	P&S	Mizzen pin rail	69.	Truss pendants	P&S	Cleat on mast
				70.	Nave line	P&S	Cleat on mast
Mizzen royal sail				71.	Jeers	P&S	Main jeer bitts
19.	Lifts	P&S	Mizzen lower top	72.	Outer tricing lines	P&S	Main pin rail
20.	Ties and halliards	P&S	Mizzen lower top	73.	Inner tricing lines	P&S	Main shroud cleat
21.	Braces	P&S	Mizzen lower top	74.	Braces	P&S	Cleat on bulwark
22.	Clew lines	P&S	Mizzen shroud cleat	75.	Lifts	P&S	Main pin rail
23.	Bowlines	P&S	Main lower top	76.	Leech lines	P&S	Barricade in the waist
24.	Sheets	P&S	Mizzen shroud cleat	77.	Bunt lines	P&S	Barricade at the forecastle
				78.	Clew garnets	P&S	Outer sheave main topsail sheet bitts
Mizzen staysail				79.	Sheets	P&S	Gun deck–cleat
25.	Halliard	S	Cleat at bulwark	80.	Tacks	P&S	Gun deck–cleat
26.	Downhauler	S	Main jeer bitts	81.	Bowlines	P&S	Main topsail sheet bitts gun deck
27.	Sheets	P&S	Mizzen pin rail	82.	Slablines	P&S	Main topsail sheet bitts gun deck
28.	Brails	P&S	Mizzen shroud cleat				
				Main topsail			
Mizzen topmast staysail				83.	Lifts	P&S	Barricade in the waist
29.	Halliard	P	Mizzen channel–mizzen pin rail	84.	Halliards	P	Main jeer bitts
30.	Downhauler	P	Main jeer bitts	85.	Braces	P&S	Main shroud cleat
31.	Sheets	P&S	Mizzen channel–mizzen pin rail	86.	Clew lines	P&S	Barricade in waist
32.	Tacks	P&S	Main pin rail	87.	Reef tackles	P&S	Barricade in waist
				88.	Bunt lines	P&S	Barricade in waist
Mizzen topgallant staysail				89.	Bowlines	P&S	Main topsail sheet bitts gun deck
33.	Halliard	S	Mizzen pin rail	90.	Sheets	P&S	Main topsail sheet bitts gun deck
34.	Downhauler	S	Main jeer bitts				
35.	Sheets	P&S	Mizzen jeer bitts	*Main topgallant sail*			
36.	Tacks	P&S	Main top rail	91.	Lifts	P&S	Main pin rail
				92.	Halliards	S	Main pin rail
Driver							
37.	Throat halliard	S	Middle pin rail	*Main topgallant sail*			
38.	Peak halliard	P	Middle pin rail	93.	Braces	P&S	Middle pin rail
39.	Vangs	P&S	Cleat at transom	94.	Clew lines	P&S	Middle pin rail
40.	Boom sheets	P&S	Cleat at transom	95.	Bowlines	P&S	Made fast in main top
41.	Guys	P&S	Hooked to eyebolt in quarter piece	96.	Sheets	P&S	Main shroud cleat
42.	Topping lifts	–	Driver boom				
43.	Peak brails	P&S	Cleat on mast	*Main royal sail*			
44.	Middle brails	P&S	Mizzen shroud cleat	97.	Braces	P&S	Fore shroud leg–main topgallant shroud
45.	Throat brails	P&S	Cleat on mast	98.	Lifts	P&S	Main lower top
46.	Foot brails	P&S	Cleat on mast	99.	Clew lines	P&S	Main pin rail
47.	Sheet	–	Driver boom	100.	Bowlines	P&S	Main lower top
				101.	Sheets	P&S	Main pin rail
Jib							
48.	Stay	S	Fore jeer bitts	*Main staysail*			
49.	Halliard	S	Fore jeer bitts	102.	Halliard	S	Main jeer bitts
50.	Downhauler–inhauler (for traveller)	P	Breasthook pin rail	103.	Downhauler	S	Fore jeer bitts
51.	Sheets	P&S	Timberhead at forecastle	104.	Sheets	P&S	Main pin rail
52.	Tacks	S	Breasthook pin rail				
53.	Outhauler	S	Breasthook pin rail				

No	Item	Side	Belaying location
Main topmast staysail			
105.	Halliard	P	Main jeer bitts
106.	Downhauler	P	Fore jeer bitts
107.	Sheets	P&S	Main pin rail
108.	Tacks	P&S	Fore shroud cleat
109.	Brails	P&S	Barricade at forecastle
Main topgallant staysail			
110.	Halliard	P	Main pin rail
111.	Downhauler	–	Fore lower top rail
112.	Sheets	P&S	Main pin rail
113.	Tacks	P&S	Fore lower lip
Main studdingsail			
114.	Topping lift	P&S	Main shroud cleat
115.	Fore guy	P&S	Deck cleat forecastle
116.	After guy	P&S	Lashed to eyebolt in quarter piece
117.	Martingale	P&S	Main channel
118.	Outer halliard	P&S	Main shroud cleat
119.	Inner halliard	P&S	Main shroud cleat
120.	Fore tack	P&S	Main shroud cleat
121.	After tack	P&S	Mizzen shroud cleat
122.	Fore sheet	P&S	Main shroud cleat
123.	After sheet	P&S	Mizzen shroud cleat
Main topmast studdingsail			
124.	Topping lift	P&S	Main pin rail
125.	Brace	P&S	Mizzen shroud cleat
126.	Halliard	P&S	Main shroud cleat
127.	Tack	P&S	Mizzen shroud cleat
128.	Fore sheet	P&S	Main shroud cleat
129.	After sheet	P&S	Mizzen shroud cleat
130.	Downhauler	P&S	Fore skid beam
Main topgallant studdingsail			
131.	Halliard	P&S	Mizzen shroud cleat
132.	Tack	P&S	Main channel
133.	Fore sheet	P&S	Made fast to main topsail yard
134.	After sheet	P&S	Shroud in main lower top
Fore course			
135.	Truss pendants	P&S	Fore mast cleats
136.	Nave line	–	Fore mast cleat
137.	Jeers	P&S	Fore topsail sheet bitts
138.	Outer tricing lines	P&S	Fore shroud cleat
139.	Inner tricing lines	P&S	Fore shroud cleat
140.	Braces	P&S	Main jeer bitts
141.	Lifts	P&S	Barricade at forecastle
142.	Leech lines	P&S	Barricade at forecastle
143.	Bunt lines	P&S	Barricade at forecastle
144.	Clew garnets	P&S	Outer sheave fore topsail sheet bitts
145.	Sheets	P&S	Cleat–gun deck
146.	Tacks	P&S	Cleat at cathead
147.	Bowlines	P&S	Forecastle rail
148.	Slablines	P&S	Fore topsail sheet bitts
Fore topsail			
149.	Lifts	P&S	Fore shroud cleat
150.	Halliards	P&S	Fore channel to timberhead at forecastle
151.	Braces	P&S	Fore skid beams
152.	Clew lines	P&S	Fore shroud cleat
153.	Reef tackles	P&S	Fore jeer bitts
154.	Bunt lines	P&S	Fore shroud cleat
155.	Bowlines	P&S	Fore jeer bitts
156.	Sheets	P&S	Fore jeer bitts
Fore topgallant sail			
157.	Lifts	P&S	Fore lower top
158.	Halliards	P&S	Fore lower top
159.	Braces	P&S	Barricade at forecastle
160.	Clew lines	P&S	Fore shroud cleat
161.	Bowlines	P&S	Fore lower top
162.	Sheets	P&S	Fore shroud cleat
Fore royal sail			
163.	Braces	P&S	Fore lower top
164.	Lifts	P&S	Fore lower top
165.	Bowlines	P&S	Rough-tree rail in bows
166.	Clew lines	P&S	Fore shroud cleat
167.	Sheets	P&S	Fore shroud cleat
Fore staysail			
168.	Halliard	S	Fore shroud cleat
169.	Downhauler	S	Fore shroud cleat
170.	Sheets	P&S	Fore shroud cleat
Fore topmast staysail			
171.	Stay	P	Fore jeer bitts
172.	Halliard	P	Fore shroud cleat
173.	Downhauler	S	Breasthook pin rail
174.	Sheets	P&S	Fore shroud cleat
175.	Outhauler	S	Breasthook pin rail
Middle staysail			
176.	Stay	S	Main jeer bitts
177.	Halliard	P	Main jeer bitts
178.	Downhauler	–	Fore lower top
179.	Sheets	P&S	Barricade in waist
180.	Tacks	P&S	Fore lower top
181.	Tricing line	P&S	Fore lower top rail
Fore studdingsail			
182.	Topping lift	P&S	Fore shroud cleat
183.	Fore guy	P&S	Timberhead at forecastle
184.	After guy	P&S	Main channel
185.	Martingale	P&S	Timberhead at forecastle
186.	Outer halliard	P&S	Rail at forecastle
187.	Inner halliard	P&S	Rail at forecastle
188.	Fore tack	P&S	Timberhead at forecastle
189.	After tack	P&S	Main channel
190.	Fore sheet	P&S	Deck cleat–gangway
191.	After sheet	P&S	Main shroud cleat
Fore topmast studdingsail			
192.	Topping lift	P&S	Deck cleat at forecastle
193.	Brace	P&S	Deck cleat at gangway
194.	Halliard	P&S	Main shroud cleat
195.	Tack	P&S	Deck cleat at gangway
196.	Fore sheet	P&S	Fore lower top
197.	After sheet	P&S	Fore shroud cleat
198.	Downhauler	P&S	Middle skid beam
Fore topgallant studdingsail			
199.	Halliard	P&S	Fore lower top rail
200.	Tack	P&S	Fore lower top rail
201.	Fore sheet	P&S	Lashed to topgallant yard
202.	After sheet	P&S	Fore lower top

Barron. *Essex*, in company with the *President, Constellation* and *Congress*, was sent to reinforce the Mediterranean Squadron and would remain there until July 1806, when she returned to the Washington Navy yard to be placed in ordinary under Commodore John Rogers.

In December of 1807, Congress authorized the building of 188 gunboats, bringing the total to 257. At the same time the Non-Importation Act went into effect and an embargo was placed on all foreign commerce. The result was a deep depression and widespread discontent, bringing the United States to near financial ruin. The embargo was lifted in March 1809 and replaced with a Non-Intercourse Act, which prohibited commerce with Britain or France.

The *Essex* remained relatively inactive, although on station, after her refit was completed in 1809 until ordered to Europe in November 1810. She was under the command of Captain John Smith and was sent bearing dispatches to France and Britain concerning the deteriorating relations between the United States and Britain. She returned to the United States the following July, and in December was again on station at Newport under Commodore John Rogers.

The 90-day embargo on all British shipping declared by President Madison in April 1812 signalled the preparations for war with Great Britain. American naval officers fitted out their ships in spite of shortages in men and materials. The *Essex* was put back onto ordinary in June at New York, to refit her masts, under the command of Master Commandant David Porter. Despite Porter's objections to her armament, the *Essex* left New York carrying forty 32pdr carronades and six long 12pdrs. The repairs to the *Essex* delayed her departure from New York as part of Commodore John Roger's squadron. Porter was instructed to proceed south in search of the British frigate *Thetis*, then to use his judgement in departing from those orders if necessary. From 11 July to 13 August, when Porter captured the 20-gun sloop of war *Alert*, he cruised north to Newfoundland. On 12 September he completed his first cruise with the capture of several small British vessels and returned to the Washington Navy yard for minor repairs.

Porter's second cruise would take him to the Pacific. The Navy had been organized into three squadrons, each composed of two frigates and a sloop of war. The *Essex* was to join Commodore William Bainbridge's squadron of the *Constitution* and the *Hornet*; sailing singly or together, they were to proceed to the Cape Verde islands, back across the Atlantic to the Island of Fernando de Noronha, then south to Brazil. Depending on circumstances, they could then head for St Helena or the South Atlantic to seek British whalers in the Pacific.

After stopping at Noronha and leaving word for Commodore Bainbridge in December of 1813, Porter rounded The Horn into the Pacific Ocean. From March of that year until September he captured fourteen British whalers. The 8-gun *Atlantic*, captured early in May, was refitted and renamed *Essex Junior*. She was placed under the command of Lieutenant Downes who was then given sixty men. The *Essex* and *Essex Junior* left the Island of Nukahiva on 12 December bound for the harbour of Valparaiso.

In February 1814 the *Essex* and her consort arrived at Valparaiso, only to have the British frigate *Phoebe*, Captain James Hillyar, and HM Sloop *Cherub* appear off the neutral port. Porter left the *Essex Junior* on patrol while he brought the *Essex* into port. Weeks of taunts followed between the two adversaries, while the two British ships replenished supplies. Porter tried in vain to bring Hillyar to a single ship duel. Then on 25 February, Porter towed his two prizes, the *Hector* and the *Catherine*, out into the harbour and burned them.

From that day forward Hillyar kept the entrance to the habour well blockaded. In late March Porter concluded that he must try to make a break for open water. On the 28th he put on all sail, but a vicious squall confronted him, carrying away his main topmast. As the *Phoebe* and *Cherub* closed in, Porter ran the *Essex* into a small bay some miles from the city and 'within pistol shot' of shore, dropped anchor. Porter's worst fears were realized when *Phoebe* positioned herself beyond the range of Porter's carronades. With the *Phoebe* off her stern and the *Cherub* off her bow, Porter could only run three of his long guns out the stern windows. After three hours of determined fighting the *Essex* struck her colours.

CAREER SUMMARY
FIRST COMMISSIONED OFFICER CAPTAIN EDWARD PREBLE
1799

December 22	Sailed from Salem to join the Frigate *Congress* at Newport, Rhode Island.
December 27	Arrived Newport – completed ship's complement of marines.

1800

January 7	Sailed for Batavia and Java with *Congress*, convoying three merchant vessels.
January 11	Parted with the three merchant vessels.
January 13	Heavy gales 24 hours. Shipped water down fore hatchway. Bored holes in waterways below decks to clear water.
January 14	Repaired storm damage to rigging.
January 16	Storm carried away one main shroud.
January 17	Repaired sails and rigging.
January 24	Main mast sprung between decks. Secured main mast and rigging.
January 25	Main trestletrees broken; fished and woolded main mast. Set up preventer shrouds.
February 7	First American warship to cross the equator.
February 14	Lost two able seamen overboard. Dismounted two quarter-deck guns and stowed them below.
March 18	(Harbour of Table Bay) repaired rigging.
March 28	Got up topmasts and yards.
March 28	First American warship to round the Cape of Good Hope.
March 29	Strong gales carried away main trusses, preparing more.
May 6	At anchor Claps Island. Saw sail, fired two guns, gave chase. Brought ship to anchor, found her American ship commanded by a Frenchman. Took out our officers and men. Ship condemned.
May 15	Anchored off Onrust Isle. Fired 16-gun salute, answered from fort. Captain preble went ashore in the barge.
May 18	Anchored at Batavia Roads. Draught of water 18ft forward, 18ft 11in aft.
July 1	Proceeded to sea with 14 sail under convoy to the United States.
September 15	At anchor at Island of St Helena Roads.
November 28	Arrived at New York. Four sick on board.
December 25	Moored in Wallabout Bay on Long Island side. Mainmast taken out and replaced—new gang of main shrouds. Kept 35 of crew to keep the ship. New boats being built for the ship. Ship placed in ordinary, Mr Phipps and Mr Lee officers in charge to be relieved by Mr Beale and Mr Tew.
December 31	Stowed sheet anchor below unstocked.

1801

February 3	Congress ratifies peace treaty with France.
April 1	Received orders to prepare the ship for 12-month cruise and sail to Hampton Roads to join squadron.
May 14	Set sail for Hampton Roads.

SECOND COMMISSIONED OFFICER CAPTAIN WILLIAM BAINBRIDGE

May 20	US ships under Commodore Dale sail to the Mediterranean for the protection of American commerce from the Barbary pirates.
July 1	Arrived at Gibraltar.
July 4	Sailed out of the Bay of Gibraltar with the ship *Grand Turk* and brig *Hope*.
July 13	Crew employed painting boats, fitting preventer braces fore and aft for lower topsail yards.
July 19	Arrived at the Bay of Tunis. Received orders to proceed to Barcelona for convoy duty through the straits of Gibraltar.
July 21	Weighed anchor. Brig *Hope* in convoy to Sicily.
July 29	Arrived at the Bay of Marseilles.
August 2	Came to anchor at Barcelona Roads. American consul came alongside but could not board.
August 3	Commenced getting ballast and water.
August 9	16 sail under convoy, one Swedish ship permitted among fleet.
August 15	At island of Plane. Saw xebec, gave chase. Brought him about, ordered him to heave to with no effect. Fired into him, hauled down his colours, found him a Morrish ship belonging to Tangiers. Dr Wells went aboard to treat wounds.
August 31	Arrived at Gibraltar.
September 1	Weighed anchor, beat out of Bay under double reefed topsails.
September 7	Came to anchor in Malaga Bay in 15 fathoms water, about 15 sail waiting in this port for convoy, now loading.
September 12	Weighed anchor sailed out of bay.
September 22	Arrived Bay of Tunis.
September 23	Came to anchor Cape Catharge.
September 25	In company with the *Philadelphia*, beating out of bay of Tunis.
September 28	Made town of Tripoli in company with *Philadelphia*.
September 29	Fired on by two gun-boats, returned shots. Went on board *Philadelphia*. Captains Barron and Bainbridge agree to leave the station.
October 25	Lying in the Bay of Malaga with a hard gale blowing. Four American vessels in this port awaiting convoy. Prepared to sail.
October 27	Brought to anchor in the Bay of Algeriras. Received provisions.
December 19	Hard gales. Took in flying jibboom. 7 pm fell in with convoy from Malaga.

1802

February 6	Congress recognized a state of war with Tripoli.
February 20	Anchored at Bay of Algeriras. Blockade duty.

June 16	Sailed from Gibraltar for New York.
July 14	Off Sandy Hook. Commenced painting ship's sides.
July 15	Gale carried away main topmast, main and fore topgallant yards split, main topgallant and two seamen lost.
July 15	Swayed up new main topmast, topgallants.
July 23	Arrived New York. Received orders to proceed with ship to Washington.
July 29	Got ship underway and beat down.
August 2	Laid up in ordinary under sailing master Richard Butler.
August 9	Anchored below Smith's point. Pilot ran us inshore to the entrance of the Eastern Branch.

1803

October 12	Congress ratifies peace treaty with Morocco.

1804

May	*Essex* recommissioned.

THIRD COMMISSIONED OFFICER CAPTAIN JAMES BARRON

June 3	Assigned to reinforce the Mediterranean squadron.
July 4	Sailed with the *President, Congress* and *Constellation*.
August 17	Arrived at Gibraltar. Left on blockade duty until relieved by brig *Siren* (30 August).
August 30	Left Gibraltar.
November 2	Arrive at Syracuse harbour.

1805

February 4	Sailed to Malta with Commodore Samuel Barron seriously ill.
March 3	Ordered to sail to Venice to obtain a bomb vessel.
March 21	Impossible to cross the bar at Venice.

FOURTH COMMISSIONED OFFICER CAPTAIN GEORGE COX

May	Ordered to Syracuse to pick up Tobias Lear.
May 29	Colonel Lear, Commodore John Rogers aboard *Essex* in Tripoli harbour. Raised white flag, answered by Pasha.
June 3	Peace treaty signed with Tripoli. Prisoners aboard the *Constitution* released. No further tribute paid to Tripoli.

FIFTH COMMISSIONED OFFICER CAPTAIN CHARLES STEWART

July 6	Charles Stewart appointed commanding officer.

SIXTH COMMISSIONED OFFICER CAPTAIN HUGH G CAMPBELL

August 22	Ordered to remain on station at Tunis.
September 5	Sailed from Tunis to Algeciras. Cruised this port, Tangier, Gibraltar and Cadiz until 30 May 1806.

1806

April	Congress enacted a law prohibiting importation of British goods.
May 30	Exchanged ships with Commodore John Rogers of the *Constitution*.
June 4	Sailed from Gibraltar to Washington.

July 25	Off the Delaware Capes.
July 28	Arrived at Washington. Laid up in ordinary to February 1809.
November 21	Napoleon issued Berlin Decree prohibiting trade between neutrals and Great Britain; US exempt.

1807

January 7	Great Britain decreed no neutral ships could sail between French ports.
July 2	President Jefferson ordered armed British ships out of US ports as result of *Leopard–Chesapeake* action.
November 11	Great Britain decreed neutral nations could not trade with France and her allies unless tribute was paid to Britain.
December 11	Napoleon's Milan Decree — all neutral ships paying tribute to Britain subject to confiscation by France.
December 14	Non-Importation act went into effect.
December 22	US declares embargo on all foreign commerce.

1808

April 17	Napoleon issues Bayonne Decree. American ships in violation of embargo seized.

1809

January 9	President authorized to recommission the *Essex*.

SEVENTH COMMISSIONED OFFICER CAPTAIN CHARLES STEWART

February 10	Stewart takes command. Change in armament to eighteen 32pdr carronades on the quarterdeck and forecastle.

EIGHTH COMMISSIONED OFFICER CAPTAIN JOHN SMITH

March 31	Smith takes command. *Essex* placed on station at Hampton Roads, Virginia.

1810

January 2	Napoleon instructs King of Naples (Murat) to seize all American ships and their cargoes.
February 2	Letter from Captain John Smith to Secretary of Navy Hamilton about fitting twenty-four 32pdr carronades and slides on the orlop (gun) deck.
March 23	Napoleon signs Rambouillet Decree. All US ships seized prior to 20 May 1809 condemned as prizes and could be sold.
May 1	Non-Intercourse Act 1809 suspended with proviso for reapplication should France or Great Britain again disrupt US commerce.
November	On station at Hampton Roads. Ordered to Europe with dispatches relating to deteriorating relations with Great Britain.
December 4	Entered L'Orient.

1811

January 12	Arrived in England with dispatches for William Pinkney, returned to France for return dispatches, then on to Cowes, Isle of Wight, to pick up Pinkney and family to return to the US.
March 2	Non-Intercourse act invoked against Great Britain.

NINTH COMMISSIONED OFFICER MASTER COMMANDANT DAVID PORTER

August 9	Porter takes command.
October 12	Captain Porter writes Secretary of the Navy Hamilton objecting to the use of carronades aboard the *Essex*.
December	*Essex* on winter station at Newport, Rhode Island, under Commodore John Rogers.

1812

June 18	War declared with Great Britain.
June 22	Repairs at New York Navy Yard. Caulked inside and out. Copper repaired; both sides hove out. Removed masts. Main-mast altered for foremast. New main and mizzen masts installed.
July 2	David Porter promoted to Captain.
July 3	Sailed from New York. Ordered to St Augustine in search of *Thetis*.
July 11	Cut out transports *Samuel* and *Sarah* from a convoy of 7 protected by brig sloop *Nimrod*. Ransomed for $12,000.
July 13	Brig *Lamprey* captured. Sent to Baltimore as a prize.
July 26	Captured brig *Leander* off Newfoundland. Dispatched as a prize.
Aguust 2	Captured ship *Nancy* and brig *Hero* off Newfoundland, dispatched as a prize.
August 3	Captured and burned the brig *Brothers* in the Atlantic.
August 7	Brig *King George* captured and sent to Boston as a prize.
August 9	Brig *Mary* captured and sent back to the US with prisoners from previous captures.
August 13	Captured HMS *Alert* (16 guns) in the Atlantic; sent to St Johns with Captain Laugharne with promise to send her later to US.
September 4	Chased by British squadron, but eluded them.
September 7	Passed Delaware Capes into Washington Navy Yard for minor repairs.
October 6	Ordered to join squadron under Commodore William Bainbridge and to rendezvous at St Helena.
October 27	Departed Delaware Capes on cruise to Pacific for attacks on British whaling fleet.
October 30	Moved crew's berths to the gun deck. Exercised crew at the guns.
November 3	Sent up royal masts.
November 4	Got new suit of sails.
November 23	Crossed the equator.
November 24	Spoke to a Portuguese ship from Madeira; informed that a British frigate was bound to the Cape of Good Hope.
November 27	Between Isles Mayo and St Jago. Sent Lieutenant Downes ashore for word from Commodore Bainbridge.
December 2	Procuring water and provisions.
December 12	Off Brazil captured British packet *Noctor* with $55,000.

December 13	Dispatched prizes under command of Lieutenant Finch with 17 prisoners and 17 of *Essex* crew.
December 14	Made Island of Nronka. Received Bainbridge's instructions. Left a reply.
December 29	Captured and burned merchant schooner *Elizabeth* of Rio de Janeiro.

1813

February 14	Rounded Cape Horn. First American Warship to enter the Pacific Ocean.
March 14	Reached Valparaiso. Replenished supplies.
March 23	Put to sea.
March 25	Captured Peruvian schooner *Nereyda*. This ship had captured two American whalers and crews off Chile. Porter had their guns thrown overboard and the ship returned commanded by her own crew with a letter of explanation to the Spanish Viceroy.
April 5	Re-captured American whaler *Barclay*, a prize of *Nereyda* off Peru. Returned to her captain and sailed in consort with the *Essex*.
April 29	Captured *Montezuma, Policy, Georgiana* (Letters of Marque) with boat parties from the *Essex*.
May 29	*Essex* and her prize *Georgiana* captured whalers *Atlantic, Greenwich, Rose, Hector* and *Catherine*.
June 13	Captured whalers *Charlton, Seringapatam, New Zealander. Seringapatam* was recaptured by her own crew. *New Zealander* was re-captured by HMS *Belvidera* in 1814.
August 13	Captured the Whaler *Sir Andrew Hammond* off Galapagos Island.
October 19	Claimed the Marquesas Islands for the US. Established a base for repairs to the *Essex*, built a fort and overcame the inhabitants.
December 12	Sailed from Nukahiva with the *Essex Junior*, ex-*Atlantic*.

1814

February 3	Entered harbour of Valparaiso. Made minor repairs. *Essex Junior* under Lieutenant Downes sent to patrol the entrance to the habour.
February 9	British frigate *Phoebe* and the sloop *Cherub* sighted at the entrance to the harbour by the *Essex Junior*. Blockaded by the British vessels.
February 25	Prizes *Catherine* and *Hector* burned in Valparaiso harbour.
March 28	*Essex* captured by *Phoebe*, Captain Hillyar, and *Cherub* in Valparaiso harbour. *Essex*: 58 killed, 31 drowned, 66 wounded; British vessels: 5 killed, 10 wounded.
April 27	*Essex Junior* sailed to the US with Captain Porter and paroled Americans.
May 31	The *Essex* and *Phoebe* left Valparaiso in company.
August 4	Arrived at Rio de Janeiro for repairs to the *Essex*. Commissioned as HMS *Essex*.
September 15	Sailed in company with HMS *Nereus* and *Phoebe*.
November 13	Anchored in Plymouth sound. Dismantled. Tied up as a hulk. (She was used as a convict ship from October 1823 and not sold until 6 July 1837).

SOURCES

INSTITUTIONS

National Archives, Washington, DC. Hackett draught 41-9-1L.
Library of Congress, Washington DC. Thomas Jefferson papers. CXLVI Fol 254111 *Essex* condition 1805.
Essex Institute, Salem, MA. Scrapbooks on William Hackett — Shipbuilding.
United States Naval Academy Museum, Annapolis, Maryland.
Peabody Museum, Salem, Massacusetts.
Petersborough Historical Society, Petersborough, New Hampshire.
Portsmouth Historical Society, Portsmouth, New Hampshire.

PUBLICATIONS AND BOOKS

The Frigate Essex Papers: Building the Salem Frigate 1798–99, Philip Chadwick Foster Smith, published by Peabody Museum of Salem (Salem, Mass 1974).
Naval Documents Related to the Quasi-War Between the United States and France, published by the Government Printing Office (Washington DC 1935–45), 7 vols.
Naval Documents Related to the United States Wars with the Barbary Powers, published by the Goverment Printing Office (Washington DC 1939–45), 7 vols.
Journal of a Cruise Made to The Pacific Ocean, by Captain David Porter, in the Years 1812 and 1814, published by Wiley & Halsted (New York 1822), 2nd edition, 2 vols.
Port of Portsmouth Ships and the Cotton Trade 1783–1929, Ray Brighton, published by The Portsmouth Marine Society, Publication Ten (Portsmouth NH 1986).
The Checkered Career of Tobias Lear, Ray Brighton, published by The Portsmouth Marine Society, Publication Four (Portsmouth NH).
'Shipbuilding' article in *Encyclopedia of Arts, Science, and Miscellaneous Literature* (London 1797), pp 365–438.
Shipbuilder's Repository (London 1789).
Treatise on Ship-building, Mungo Muray (London 1765).
Shipwright's Vade Mecum, David Steel (London 1805).
Mastmaking, Rope-making, Sail-making, Block-making, Rigging, Seamanship, Naval Tactics, etc, David Steel (London 1794), 2 vols.
The Young Sea Officer's Sheet Anchor, Darcy Lever (London 1808).
The Masting and Rigging of English Ships of War 1625–1860, James Lees, published by Conway Maritime Press (London 1979).
'The Designs of Our First Frigates', MV Brewington, *American Neptune* Vol 8 (1948).

CORRESPONDENCE

Commander Kenneth A Johnson, USN
Mr Richard L Eddy
Mr Philip Chadwick Foster Smith

Although numerous models of the *Essex* exist, few have been built based on the lines of William Hackett. Those which have are now held in private and corporate collections, or still in the hands of the builders themselves. It is through their generosity that we are able to present photographs of models of the *Essex* here. The modelmakers are as follows:

Dr Robert J Dowst — fully rigged model.

Joseph Francella — profile view.

William Amour — model completed to the gun deck, looking aft from the bow; and planked port side view showing the gun deck under construction.

Dr William Brown — deck details of the waist, athwartship view.

Richard L Eddy — view of the spar deck framing.

2. Portrait of Wiliam Hackett by an
unknown artist. *The Peabody Museum
of Salem*

3. Captain Edward Preble, USN. Engraved
by T Kelly from the portrait in Faneuil
Hall, Boston. *Author's collection*

4. Captain David Porter, USN. *Author's collection*

5. Captain William Brainbridge, USN. *Author's collection*

6. 'Capture of the US Frigate *Essex* by His BM Frigate *Phoebe* & Sloop *Cherub* in the bay of Valparaiso.' Painting by George Ropes. *The Peabody Museum of Salem*

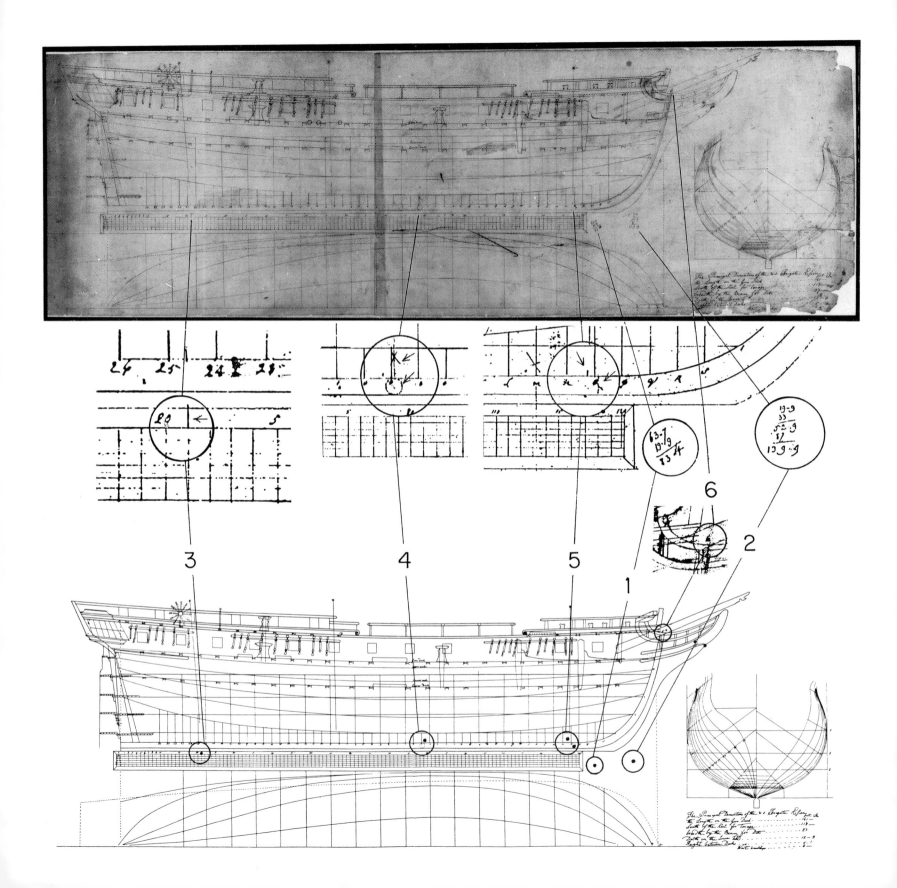

7. Opposite: The Hackett draught
1 After body calculations (preliminary)
2 Fore and after body calculations
(combined)
3 Final location of the first cant frame aft
4 Midship symbol and indicated room
and space
5 Location of boxing of the stem
6 Number 5 at the top of the stem
*Photo of the Hackett draught courtesy
of the National Archives. Lines plan
below from* Naval Documents Related to
the United States Wars with the Barbary
Powers.

8. 6pdr gun from a Massachussetts privateer
scuttled by her crew in 1779. This type is
similar to those used on the quarterdeck
of the *Essex. Author's collection*

9. Example of a pistol used during the later
part of the eighteenth century. Not seen
in the photograph is the gun hook on the
opposite side. The bolt which fastens the
cock also held the hook in line with the
barrel of the gun. Unlike the small arms
issued to the enlisted men, officers
owned their own weapons, and were
responsible for their care and
maintenance. The pistol shown was the
property of Commodore Oliver Hazard
Perry. *By courtesy of the United States
Naval Academy, Annapolis*

10. Officer's sword belonging to
Commodore Edward Preble. *By
courtesy of the US Naval Academy
Museum*

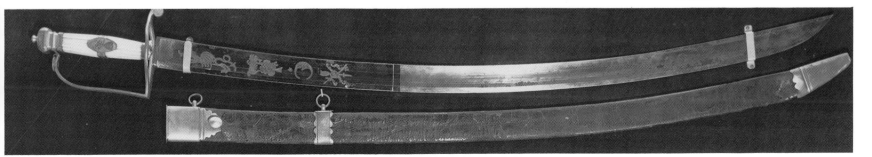

11. Rigged model of the *Essex* showing the influence of the Howard painting. *By courtesy of Dr Robert J Dowst*

12. Model of the *Essex* based on the lines by William Hackett. *By courtesy of Mr Joseph Francella. Photograph by George Ancona*

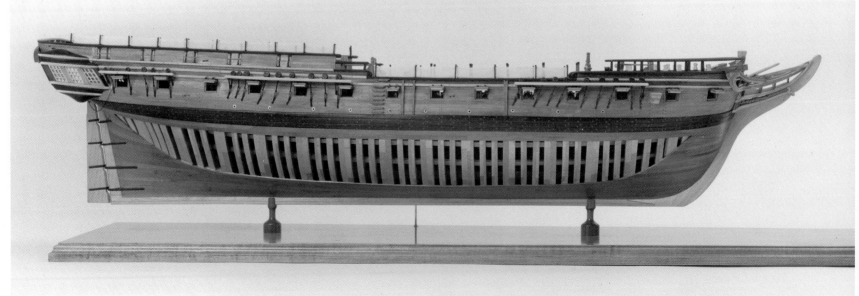

13. The beauty of the bow curves is clearly shown in this model under construction by William Amour. The darkened area at the stern will contain the great cabin. *By courtesy of Wiliam Amour. Photograph by Wiener Inc*

14. The same model from the port side showing some of the deck detail, the upper planking, wales and quarter gallery outboard. The noticeable tumblehome is evident in the quarterdeck bulwarks. *By courtesy of William Amour. Photograph by Weiner Inc*

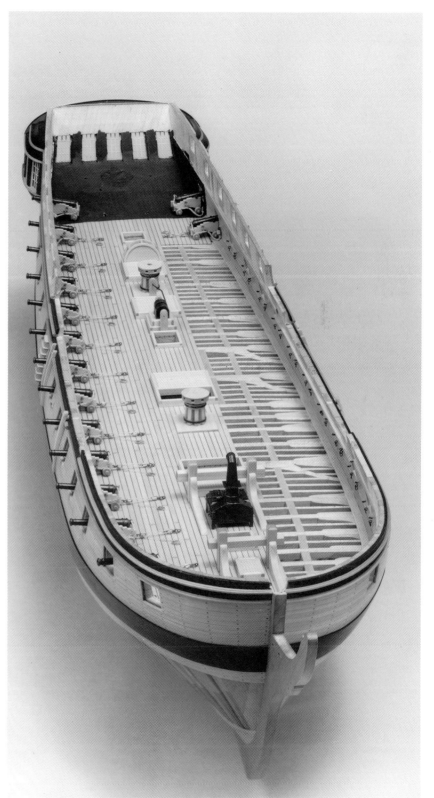

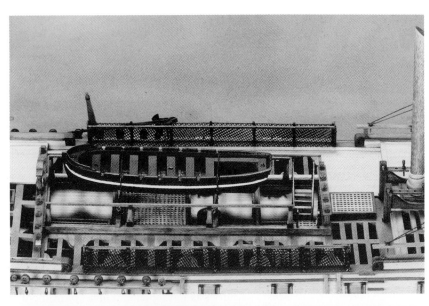

15. A port side view of the longboat stowed on the skid beams in the waist. A grating has been let into the beams for access to the boat. *By courtesy of Dr William Brown*

16. View of the spar deck with most of the framing exposed. *By courtesy of Richard L Eddy. Photograph by J Blankenship*

THE DRAWINGS

Information for all the reconstructed drawings of the frigate *Essex* came from two major sources, the draught by William Hackett and Philip C F Smith's book, *The Frigate Essex Papers*, published in 1974 by the Peabody Museum at Salem. Secondary sources include the author's own research on this vessel and similar types of the period, gathered over more than a decade. Several of the secondary sources include information, often lost in the literature, from articles and notes in periodicals, journals and historical society publications.

Early works on naval architecture illuminated the source of Hackett's information and made possible many of the constructional details, and confirm those referred to in Smith's book. The appendices in *The Frigate Essex Papers* were of inestimable value, for otherwise elusive details such as the painted and varnished fan-back chairs in the wardroom – two of them with arms – as listed in the purser's indent.

The painting, believed to be of the *Essex*, in the Peabody Museum was the source for the design for the figurehead, as noted above. This painting has long been an influence on popular impressions of the *Essex*. The artist's interpretation of the quarter galleries is reflected in a number of models, despite the fact that Hackett clearly indicated the shape and position of the stern knee on his draught at the centreline on his sheer elevation; this was not intended to represent an extension of the quarter board, as the painting, and consequently the models, show. This interpretation, however, has perpetuated the doubts about Hackett's abilities, as both a draughtsman and designer, from that time to the present.

In attempting the reconstruction of the Hackett drawing and its expansion into the line, framing, planking, and other related drawings, I felt it necessary to place complete faith in his capabilities as a designer and in his judgement. It was also my intent to remain as objective as possible while reconstructing the original design in more detail than had been done to date. As work progressed on the drawings it became clear that Hackett's draught was, in effect, a working drawing, developed to determine the size, number and placement of the ship's timbers through notations and calculations.

I have deviated from the normal practice of showing the half-breadth elevations viewed from above, and instead showed them viewed from below. This permits the bottom of the hull to be seen in the plating, framing, and planking diagrams.

The scale of Hackett's draught is based on ¼in = 1ft scale (1/48). Slight variations occur on his scale located below the sheer drawing. Nonetheless, his scale was crucial as a guide to the disposition of timbers. The most accurate section of this scale was used for measurements on the Hackett draught, then transposed to the new drawings using an accurate ¼in scale. The reduced drawings are in multiple reductions of the ¼in scale to suit the format of this volume.

A list of the principal sources for this work is found at the close of the Introduction. Space limitations preclude a complete bibliography.

A Lines and arrangement

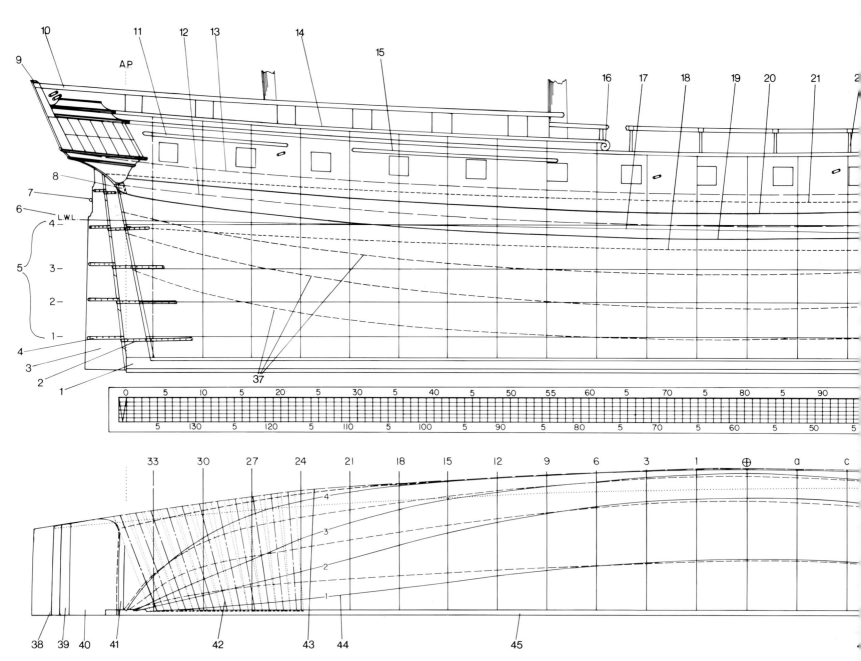

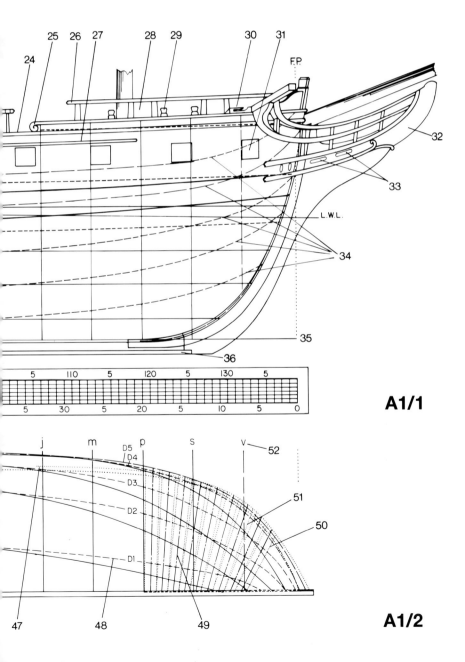

A1/1

A1/2

A Lines and arrangement

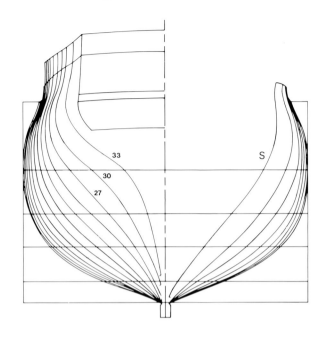

A1/3 Reconstructed body plan (1/144 scale)

33

30

27

S

A1/3

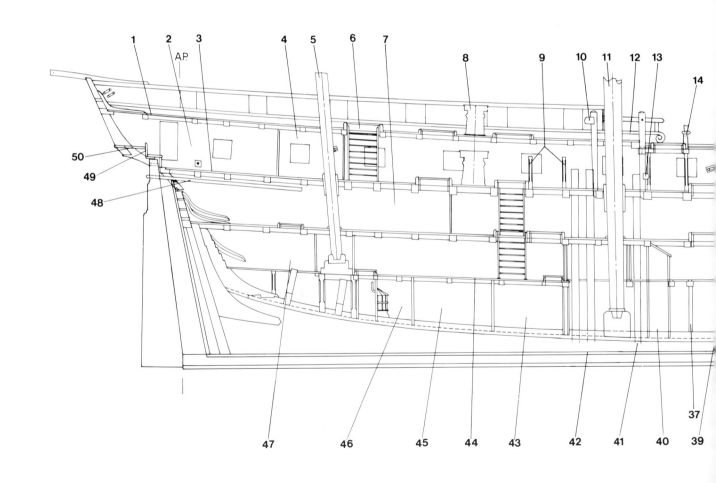

1	Quarterdeck
2	Great cabin
3	Gun deck
4	Lobby
5	Mizzen mast
6	Companionway
7	Wardroom
8	Capstan
9	Pump crank standards
10	Main jeer bitts
11	Main mast
12	Drift rail
13	Main topsail sheet bitts
14	Barricade
15	Main hatch
16	Gangboard
17	Jeer capstan spindle
18	Jeer capstan
19	Jeer capstan bed
20	Fore hatch
21	Main riding bitts
22	Belfry
23	Barricade
24	Fore jeer bitts
25	Fore mast
26	Mast hatch
27	Fore topsail sheet bitts
28	Fore riding bitts
29	Breasthook pin rail
30	Manger
31	Fore peak
32	Ladderway
33	Berth deck
34	Orlop deck (fore platform)
35	Fore hold
36	Jeer capstan spindle
37	Pillars
38	Main hold
39	Cable tier
40	Shot locker
41	Log pump
42	Chain pump boxes
43	Magazine
44	Orlop deck (after platform)
45	Filling room
46	Light room
47	Bread room
48	Tiller arm
49	Bench
50	Bench brace

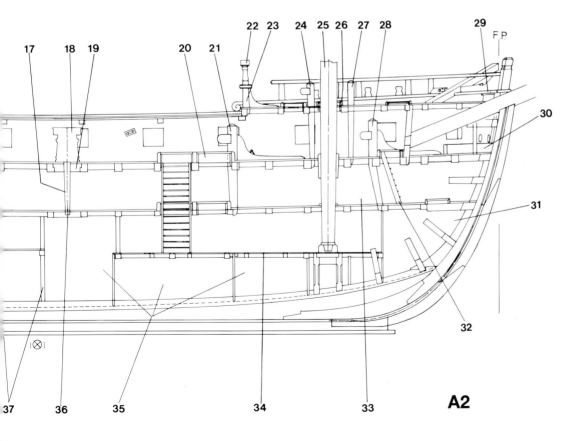

A2

35

B Hull structure

B1 **LONGITUDINAL MEMBERS (1/144 scale)**

1 After deadwood
2 Rabbet of the sternpost
3 Inner post
4 Deck transom
5 Sternpost
6 Wing transom
7 Filling transom
8 Fashion timber
9 Sternson knee
10 Crutch
11 False keel scarf
12 Scarfs of the after deadwood
13 Vertical scarf
14 Horizontal hook scarf
15 Lower futtock
16 Floor frame
17 Rabbet of the keel
18 Top of the limber board
19 Keelson
20 Forward rising wood
21 Crutch
22 Breasthook
23 Rabbet of the stem
24 Deck hook (gun deck)
25 Stemson
26 Deck hook (berth deck)
27 Apron
28 Stem
29 Forward deadwood
30 Boxing
31 Keel
32 False keel
33 Frame annotations

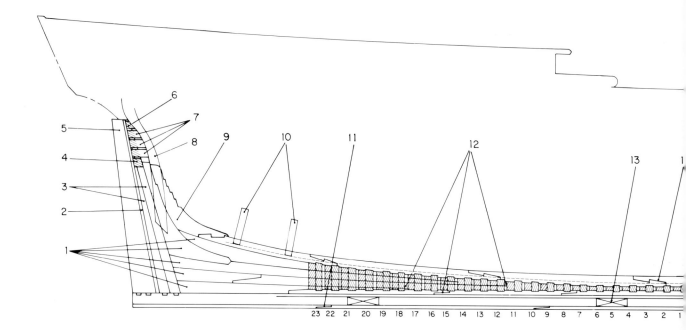

B1

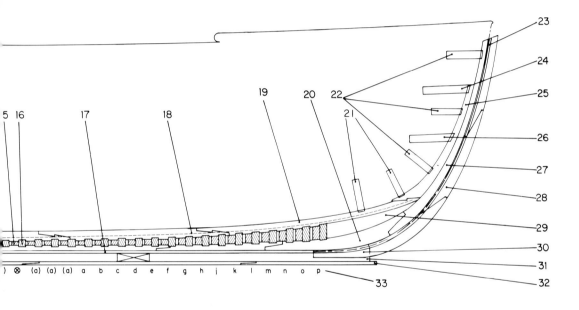

23

24

25

26

27

28

29

30

31

32

19   20   22

21

5 16   17   18

) ⊗ (a) (a) (a) a b c d e f g h j k l m n o p

33

B Hull structure

B2   FRAMING (1/144 scale)

B2/1 Sheer

B2/2 Half-breadth

1 False Keel
2 Keel
3 After deadwood
4 Sternpost
5 Fashion timber
6 After filling chocks
7 Deck transom
8 Filling transom
9 Wing transom
10 Gun deck transom
11 Seat transom
12 Window transom
13 Side counter timber
14 Vertical scarf
15 Quarterdeck transom
16 Transom timber
17 Fixed block – main and preventer brace sheave
18 Quarter gallery doorway
19 6pdr port opening
20 Rudder chain preventer bolt
21 Extended toptimber
22 12pdr port opening
23 Main sheet sheave block
24 Filling Timber
25 Upper port sill
26 Upper height of breadth
27 Bulwark timber
28 Lower port sill
29 Filling frame timber
30 Port filling block
31 Fore sheet sheave block
32 Gunwale
33 Third futtock
34 Top timber
35 Filling chocks
36 Main tack sheave block
37 Fourth futtock
38 Lower height of breadth
39 Rough-tree rail
40 Extended toptimber
41 6pdr port opening
42 Inserted timber
43 Cathead
44 Bridle port
45 Bollard timber (knighthead)
46 Stem
47 Hawse holes
48 Hawse timbers
49 Harpins
50 Boxing of the stem
51 Floor
52 Lower futtock
53 Second futtock
54 Hackett's stations
55 Toptimber
56 Waterline 4
57 Filling half timbers
58 Stern knees
59 Half timbers
60 Side counter timber

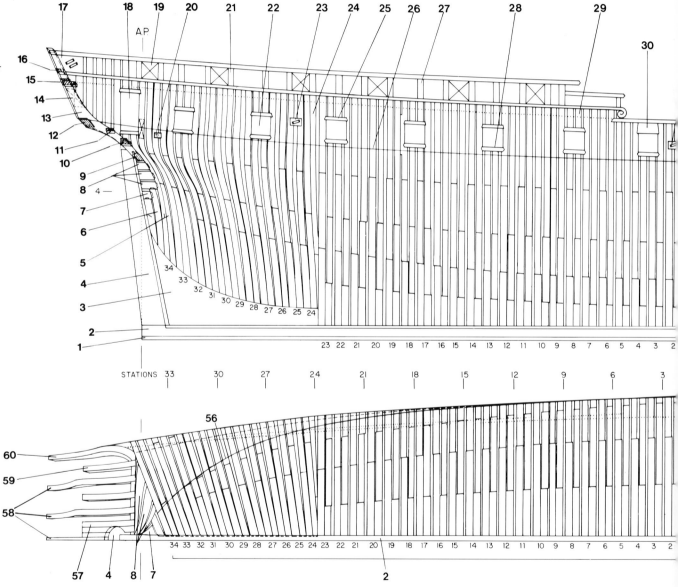

B2/1

B2/2

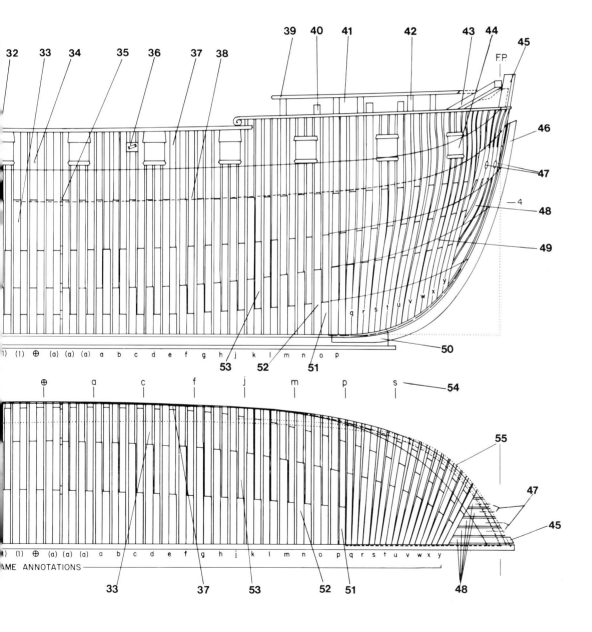

32 33 34 35 36 37 38 39 40 41 42 43 44 45

F.P.

46

47

—4
48

49

50

1) (1) ⊕ (a) (a) (a) a b c d e f g h j k l m n o p

53 52 51

q r s t u v w x y

⊕ a c f j m p s — 54

55

47

45

1) (1) ⊕ (a) (a) (a) a b c d e f g h j k l m n o p q r s t u v w x y

ME ANNOTATIONS

33 37 53 52 51 48

39

B Hull structure

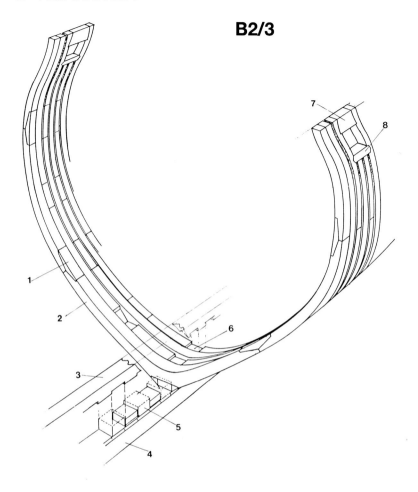

B2/3

B2/3 Perspective view of frame bend components on the keel (no scale)

1 Chock
2 Frame bend
3 Keelson
4 Keel
5 Filling chock
6 Notch for keelson
7 Port block
8 Port sill

B3 LOCATION OF FRAME BEND COMPONENTS (30 aft to cant V forward, 1/192 scale)

B3

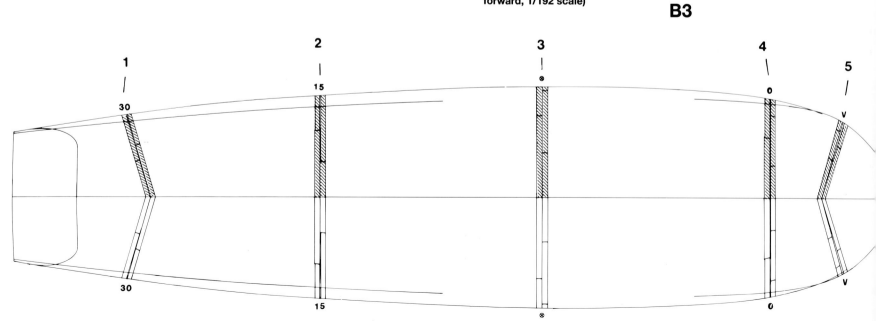

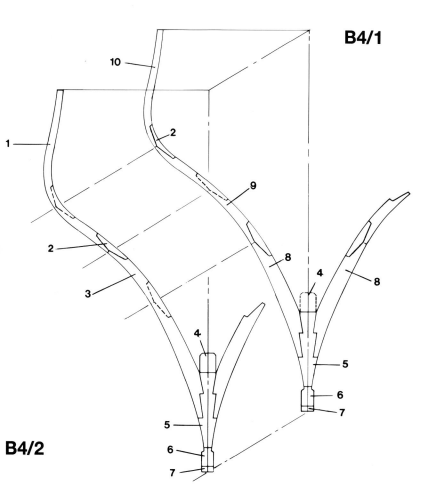

B4/1

B4/2

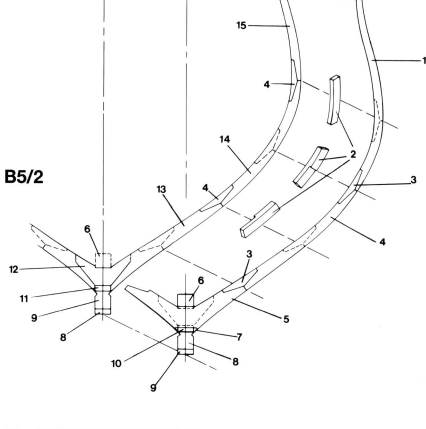

B5/1

B5/2

B4 FRAME BEND COMPONENTS (30 from aft, 1/96 scale)

B4/1 Right: Aft of joint

B4/2 Left: Forward of joint

1	Toptimber
2	Chock
3	Second futtock
4	Sternson knee
5	Deadwood
6	Keel
7	False keel
8	First futtock
9	Third futtock
10	Fourth futtock

B5 FRAME BEND COMPONENTS (15 from forward, 1/96 scale)

B5/1 Right: Forward of joint

B5/2 Left: Aft of joint

1	Fourth futtock
2	Filling chocks
3	Chock
4	Second futtock
5	Floor
6	Keelson
7	Floor chock
8	Keel
9	False keel
10	Rising wood of the floor
11	Rising wood
12	Cross chock
13	Lower futtock
14	Third futtock
15	Toptimber

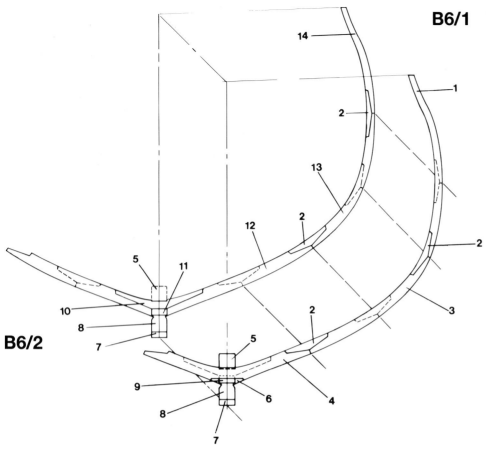

B6/1

B7 **FRAME BEND COMPONENTS (0 from forward, 1/96 scale)**

B7/1 **Right: Forward of joint**

B7/2 **Left: Aft of joint**

1	Fourth futtock
2	Filling chock
3	Chock
4	Second futtock
5	Floor
6	Keelson
7	Floor chock
8	Keel
9	False keel
10	Rising wood
11	Cross chock
12	Lower futtock
13	Third futtock
14	Toptimber
15	Timberhead of quarterdeck

B6/2

B6 **MIDSHIP BEND COMPONENTS (from forward, 1/96 scale)**

B6/1 **Right: Forward of joint**

B6/2 **Left: Aft of joint**

1	Fourth futtock
2	Chock
3	Second futtock
4	Floor
5	Keelson
6	Floor chock
7	False keel
8	Keel
9	Rising wood of the floor
10	Cross chock
11	Rising wood
12	Lower futtock
13	Third futtock
14	Toptimber

B7/1

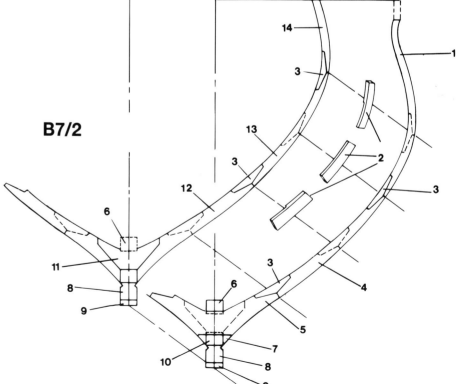

B7/2

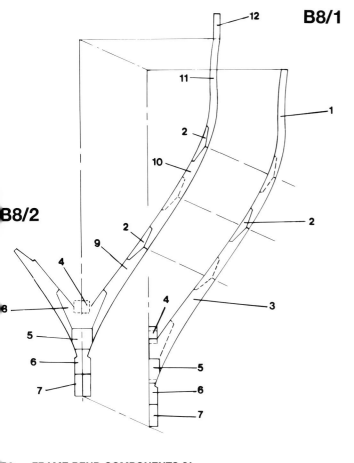

B8/1

B8/2

B8 **FRAME BEND COMPONENTS (V from forward, 1/96 scale)**

B8/1 **Right: Forward of joint**

B8/2 **Left: Aft of joint**

1 Fourth futtock
2 Chock
3 Second futtock
4 Keelson
5 Forward deadwood
6 Stem
7 Forefoot
8 Cross chock
9 First futtock
10 Third futtock
11 Toptimber
12 Timberhead

B9/1

B9 **STERN STRUCTURE (1/96 scale)**

B9/1 **Stern timbers from aft**

1 Stern knees
2 Taffrail
3 Necking transom
4 Rough-tree rail
5 Quarterdeck transom
6 Filling half timbers
7 Half timbers
8 Window transom
9 Side counter timber
10 Gun deck transom
11 Wing transom
12 Bend 34 (fashion timber)
13 After side of bend 30
14 Sternpost
15 Keel
16 False keel
17 Inner post
18 Transom chocks
19 Deck transom

20 Filling transom
21 Rabbet of the wing transom
22 Gun deck beam at bend 30
23 Quarter gallery door opening
24 Inserted timberhead

B Hull structure

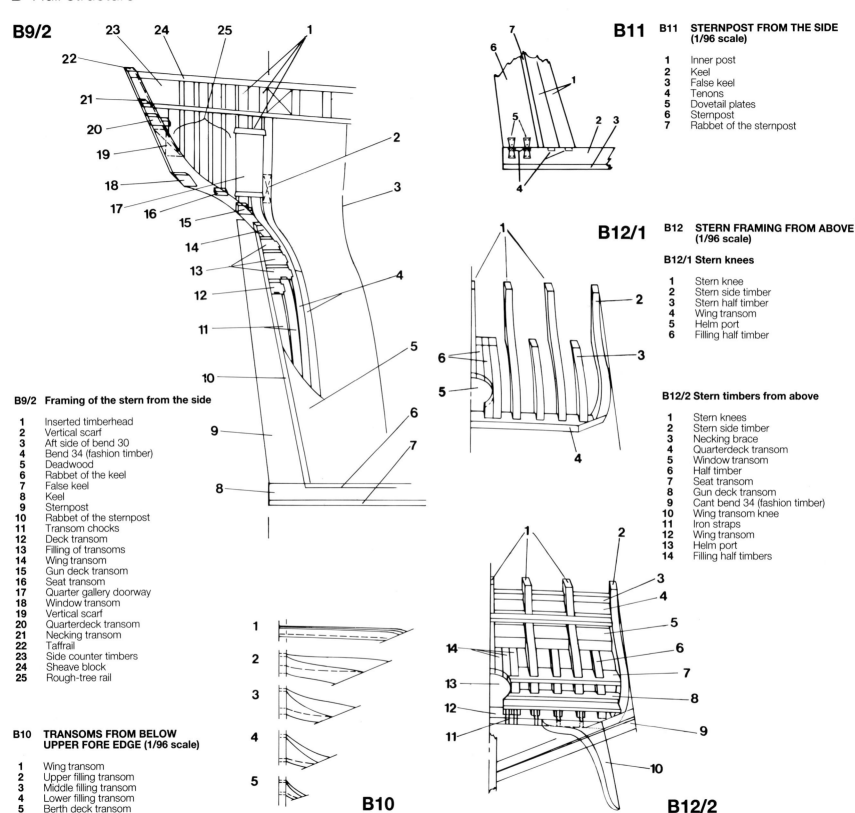

B9/2

B9/2 Framing of the stern from the side

1 Inserted timberhead
2 Vertical scarf
3 Aft side of bend 30
4 Bend 34 (fashion timber)
5 Deadwood
6 Rabbet of the keel
7 False keel
8 Keel
9 Sternpost
10 Rabbet of the sternpost
11 Transom chocks
12 Deck transom
13 Filling of transoms
14 Wing transom
15 Gun deck transom
16 Seat transom
17 Quarter gallery doorway
18 Window transom
19 Vertical scarf
20 Quarterdeck transom
21 Necking transom
22 Taffrail
23 Side counter timbers
24 Sheave block
25 Rough-tree rail

**B10 TRANSOMS FROM BELOW
UPPER FORE EDGE (1/96 scale)**

1 Wing transom
2 Upper filling transom
3 Middle filling transom
4 Lower filling transom
5 Berth deck transom

B10

**B11 STERNPOST FROM THE SIDE
(1/96 scale)**

1 Inner post
2 Keel
3 False keel
4 Tenons
5 Dovetail plates
6 Sternpost
7 Rabbet of the sternpost

**B12 STERN FRAMING FROM ABOVE
(1/96 scale)**

B12/1 Stern knees

1 Stern knee
2 Stern side timber
3 Stern half timber
4 Wing transom
5 Helm port
6 Filling half timber

B12/2 Stern timbers from above

1 Stern knees
2 Stern side timber
3 Necking brace
4 Quarterdeck transom
5 Window transom
6 Half timber
7 Seat transom
8 Gun deck transom
9 Cant bend 34 (fashion timber)
10 Wing transom knee
11 Iron straps
12 Wing transom
13 Helm port
14 Filling half timbers

B12/1

B12/2

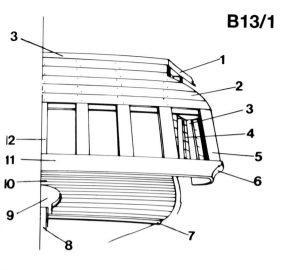

B13/1

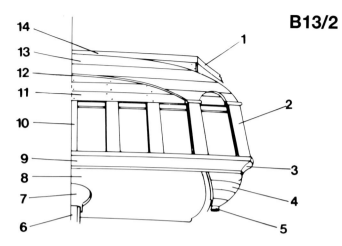

B13/2

B13/4 Profile of quarter gallery

1	Boat davit
2	Quarter gallery double hung sash light
3	Rough-tree rail
4	6pdr port opening
5	Upper finishing
6	Upper finishing rail
7	Sheer rail
8	Sheer strake
9	Moulding
10	Mizzen channel
11	Canting timber
12	12pdr port opening
13	Main wale
14	Rim rail
15	Lower stool rail
16	Sternpost
17	Rudder
18	Drop
19	Lower finishing
20	Lower counter
21	Quarter berthing
22	Lower counter rail
23	Lower counter
24	Upper counter
25	Quarter gallery false light
26	Quarter piece
27	Quarter board
28	Hollow top
29	Sheaves
30	Taffrail rife rail

B13   STERN – EXTERIOR (1/96 scale)

B13/1 Planking of the lower stern from aft

1	Rough-tree rail
2	Transom planks
3	Canting timber
4	Plank of the side
5	Quarter piece
6	Quarter berthing
7	Tuck rail
8	Sternpost
9	Helm port
10	Lower counter plank
11	Upper counter board
12	Mullion
13	Taffrail fife rail

B13/2 Upper stern planking from aft

1	Rough-tree rail
2	Quarter piece
3	Quarter berthing
4	Built-up lower finishing
5	Drop
6	Sternpost
7	Helm port
8	Lower counter
9	Upper counter
10	Mullions
11	Transon planking
12	Necking
13	Taffrail planking
14	Taffrail fife rail

B13/3 Plan of the stern – inboard of transom and quarter gallery

1	Taffrail
2	Transom knee
3	Hollow top
4	Quarter piece
5	Upper finishing rail
6	Upper finishing
7	Upper counter rail
8	Double hung sash light
9	False light
10	Canting timber
11	Rough-tree rail
12	Flat of the quarterdeck
13	Margin plank
14	Transom berthing

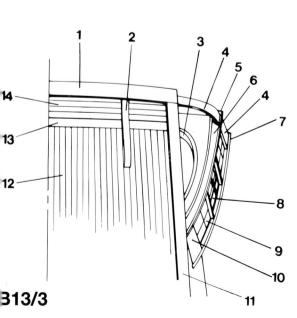

B13/3

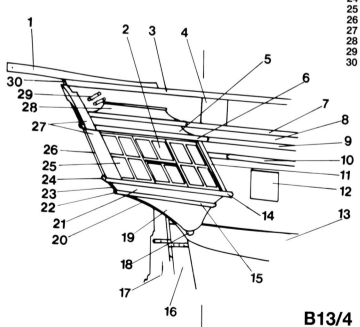

B13/4

B13/5

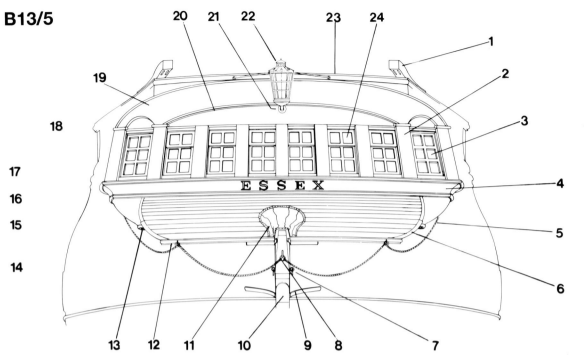

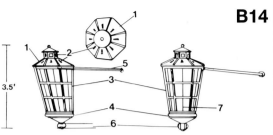

B14

B14   STERN LANTERN (1/48 scale)

1	Top
2	Air vents
3	Mullions
4	Base
5	Side brackets (copper)
6	Middle bracket (copper)
7	Copper safety wire

B13/5 Stern from aft

1	Boat davit
2	Mullion
3	Quarter gallery false light
4	Upper counter
5	Rudder preventer cable
6	Main wale
7	Preventer ringbolt
8	Copper ringbolt and thimbles
9	Gudgeon strap
10	Rudder
11	Rudder coat
12	Wing transom margin plank
13	Drop
14	Lower finishing
15	Lower counter plank
16	Lower counter rail
17	Upper counter rail
18	Quarter piece
19	Quarter board
20	Necking
21	Bracket
22	Stern lantern (tin)
23	Taffrail
24	Double hung sash light

B15   BOW STRUCTURE (1/96 scale)

B15/1 Stem timbers from the side

1	Block
2	Bobstay piece
3	Bobstay holes
4	Gammoning slots
5	Upper stem pieces
6	Main piece
7	Lower stem piece
8	Gripe
9	Horseshoe plate
10	Forefoot
11	False keel
12	Boxing of the stem
13	Deadwood
14	Keelson
15	Stemson
16	Apron
17	Rabbet of the stem
18	Mainstay collar hole
19	Gammoning knee
20	Lacing

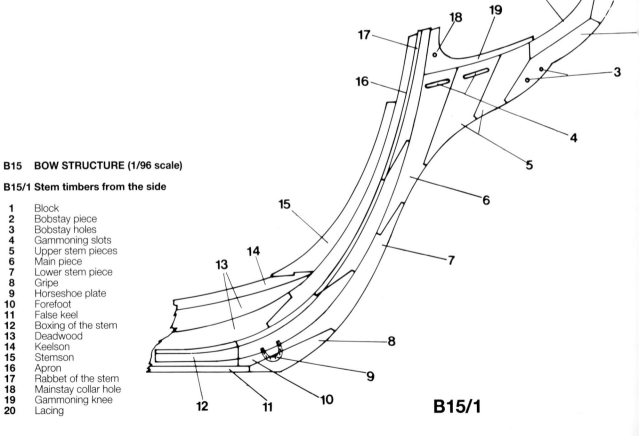

B15/1

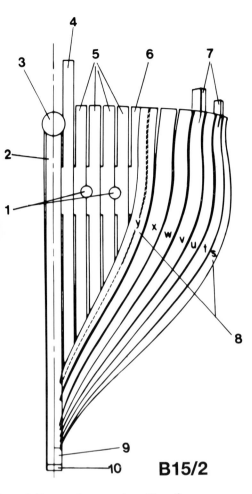

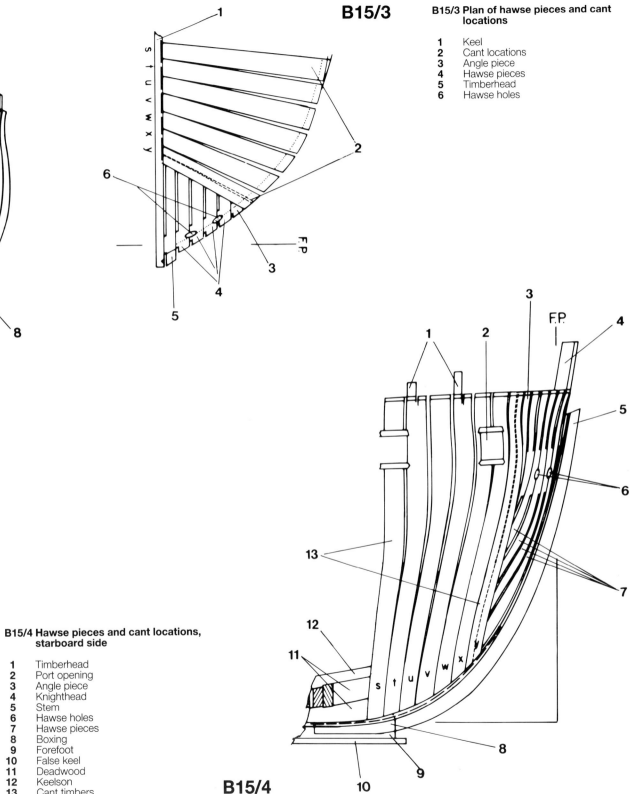

B15/3

B15/3 Plan of hawse pieces and cant locations

1 Keel
2 Cant locations
3 Angle piece
4 Hawse pieces
5 Timberhead
6 Hawse holes

B15/2 Hawse pieces and cant locations port side from forward

1 Hawse holes
2 Stem
3 Bowsprit
4 Knighthead
5 Hawse pieces
6 Angle piece
7 Timberheads
8 Cant timber locations
9 Keel
10 False keel

B15/4 Hawse pieces and cant locations, starboard side

1 Timberhead
2 Port opening
3 Angle piece
4 Knighthead
5 Stem
6 Hawse holes
7 Hawse pieces
8 Boxing
9 Forefoot
10 False keel
11 Deadwood
12 Keelson
13 Cant timbers

B15/2

B15/4

B Hull structure

B16   THE HEAD (1/48 scale)

B16/1 Starboard side, outboard

1   Horse
2   Figure block
3   Bobstay holes
4   Bobstay piece
5   Gammoning holes
6   Gammoning bolster
7   Hawse holes
8   Wash cant
9   Lower cheek
10 Bolster
11 Filling
12 Upper cheek
13 Gammoning knee
14 Cross timbers (stem)
15 Lower rail
16 Ekeing
17 Supporter
18 Forecastle planksheer
19 Cathead
20 Rough-tree rail
21 Bollard timber (knighthead)
22 Wash board
23 Boomkin knee
24 After cross timber
25 Middle cross timber
26 Fore cross timber
27 Bowsprit

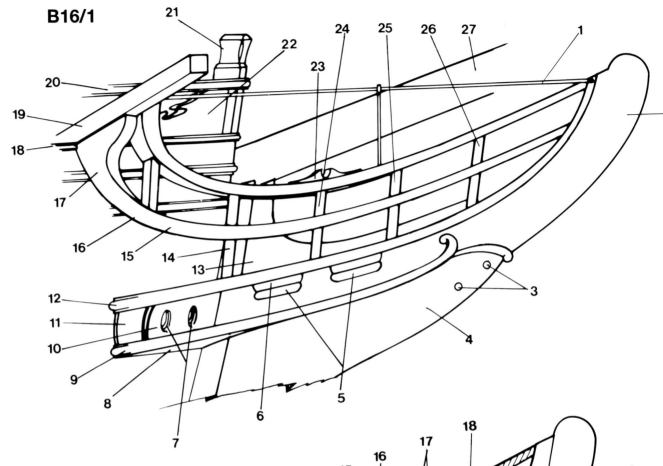

B16/1

B16/2 Inboard through the centre line

1   Block
2   Lacing
3   Middle rail
4   Fore cross timber
5   Bobstay piece
6   Middle cross timber
7   Gammoning slot
8   After cross timber
9   Hole for mainstay collar
10 Stem
11 Gammoning knee
12 Boomkin knee
13 Seat of ease
14 Seat board
15 Seat support
16 Grating
17 Coaming
18 Upper rail
19 Knee

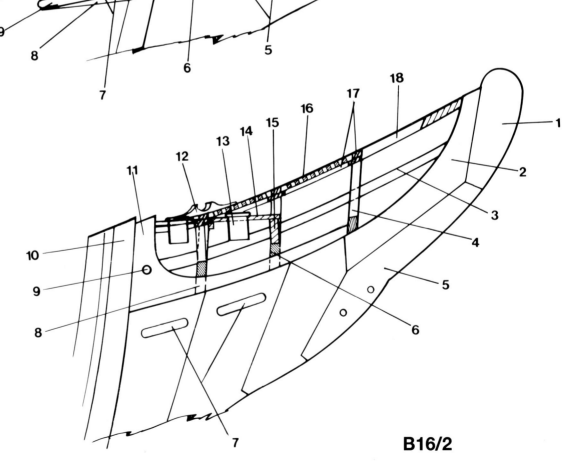

B16/2

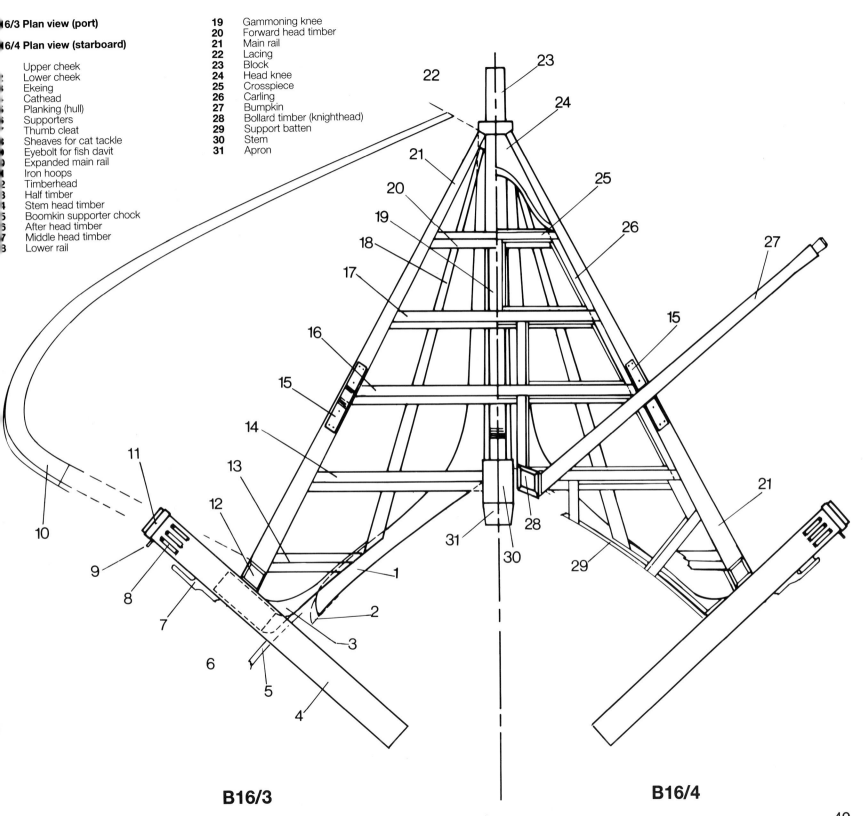

B16/3

B16/4

B Hull structure

B16/5 Gratings

1 Stem
2 Gammoning knee
3 Gammoning
4 Seat of ease
5 Bowsprit
6 Lacing
7 Block
8 Head knee
9 Lower rail
10 Upper cheek
11 Gratings
12 Boomkin knee
13 Main rail
14 Timberhead
15 Cathead
16 Ledges
17 Apron

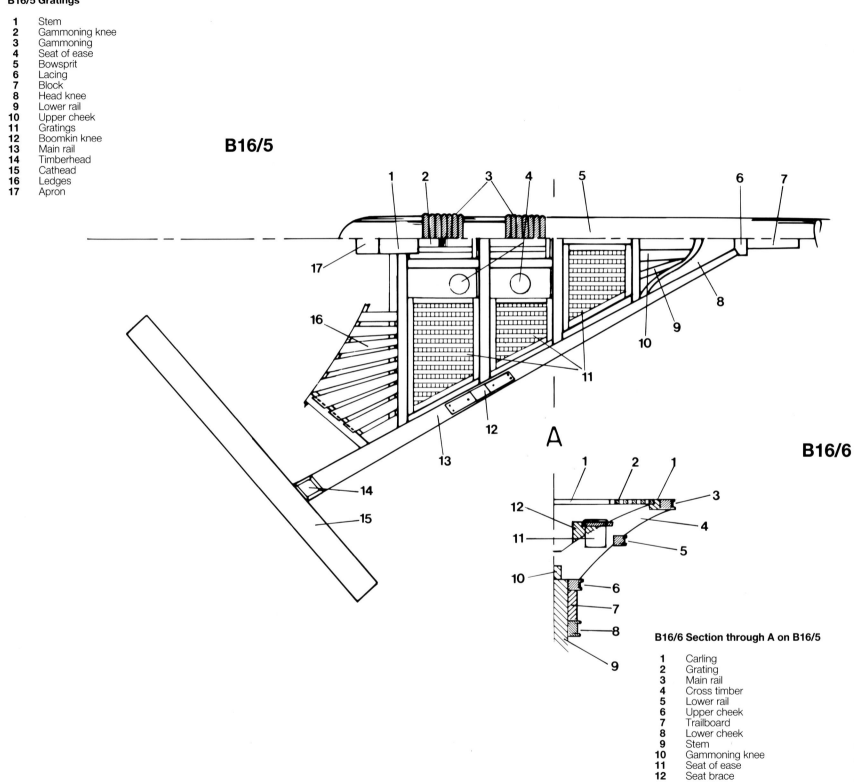

B16/5

B16/6

B16/6 Section through A on B16/5

1 Carling
2 Grating
3 Main rail
4 Cross timber
5 Lower rail
6 Upper cheek
7 Trailboard
8 Lower cheek
9 Stem
10 Gammoning knee
11 Seat of ease
12 Seat brace

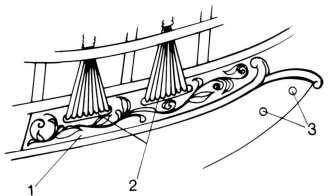

B16/7

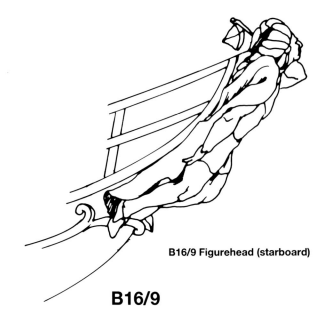

B16/9 Figurehead (starboard)

B16/9

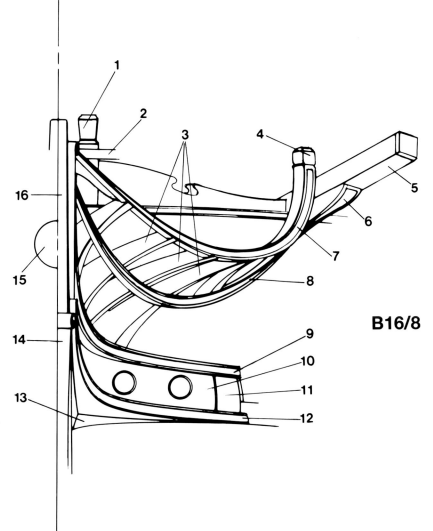

B16/8

B16/8 The head from ahead

1 Bollard timber (knighthead)
2 Rough-tree rail
3 Head timbers
4 Timberhead
5 Cathead
6 Supporter
7 Main rail
8 Ekeing
9 Upper cheek
10 Bolster
11 Filling piece
12 Lower cheek
13 Wash cant
14 Bobstay piece
15 Bowsprit hole
16 Block

C1   SECTIONS

**C1/1   Location of frame bends 30 aft to
         cant V forward (1/92 scale)**

1   Frame bend 30 from aft (starboard
         side)
2   Frame bend 15 from forward (port
         side)
3   Midship bend 0 from forward (port
         side)
4   Frame bend 0 from forward (port side)
5   Frame bend V from forward (port side)

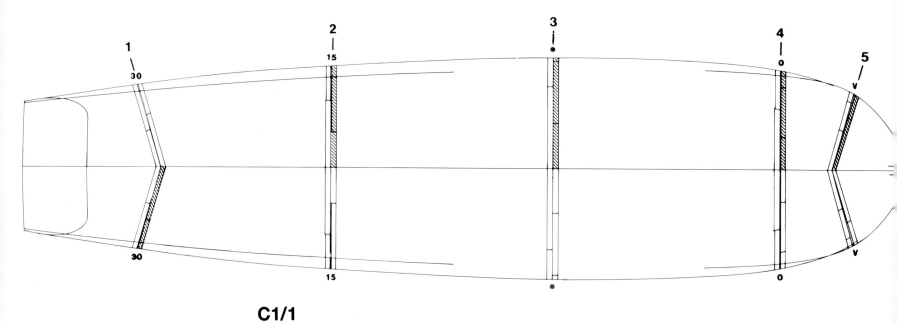

C1/1

C1/2

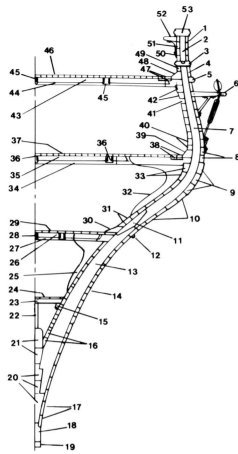

C1/3

C1/2	Frame bend 30 from forward (starboard side, 1/96 scale)		26	Ledge
			27	Berth deck beam
			28	Berth deck carling
1	Berthing		29	Berth deck plank
2	Inserted timberhead		30	Berth deck waterway
3	Planksheet		31	Berth deck spirketting
4	Sheer plank		32	Gun deck hanging knee
5	Moulding		33	Gun deck clamp
6	Mizzen channel		34	Gun deck beam
7	Fourth futtock		35	Gun deck ledge
8	Thickstuff over the wales		36	Gun deck carling
9	Main wale		37	Gun deck plank
10	Diminishing plank and thickstuff		38	Gun deck binding strakes
11	Chock		39	Gun deck waterway
12	Batten for the copper		40	Gun deck spirketting
13	Second futtock		41	Air space
14	Plank of the bottom		42	Quarterdeck clamp
15	Clamp		43	Quarterdeck ledge
16	Limber strakes		44	Quarterdeck beam
17	Garboard strakes		45	Quarterdeck carling
18	Keel		46	Quarterdeck plank
19	False keel		47	Quarterdeck binding strakes
20	Deadwood		48	Quarterdeck waterway
21	Keelson		49	Quarterdeck spirketting
22	Pillar		50	Iron knee
23	Bread room beam		51	Quarterdeck berthing
24	Bread room plank		52	Mizzen pin rail
25	Hanging knee		53	Rough-tree rail

C1/3	Frame bend 15 aft of the joint line from forward (port side, 1/96 scale)		26	False keel
			27	Rising wood
			28	Cross chock
			29	Keelson
1	Toptimber aft of bend 15		30	Magazine floor
2	Port sill		31	Limber board
3	Sheer strakes		32	Carling
4	Deadeye		33	Orlop deck beam
5	Main channel		34	Ledge
6	Channel brace (iron)		35	Clamp
7	Chain link		36	Orlop deck plank
8	Backing link		37	Lodging knee
9	Bolt benched on a ring		38	Hanging knee
10	Toe link		39	Berth deck beam
11	Toptimber		40	Hatch carling
12	Main wale		41	Headledge
13	Batten for copper		42	Grating
14	Diminishing plank and thickstuff		43	Ladderway (companionway)
15	Third futtock		44	Hatch coaming
16	Plank of the bottom		45	Berth deck plank
17	Standard		46	Binding strakes
18	Chock		47	Waterway
19	Spirketting		48	Quickwork
20	Lower futtock		49	Air space
21	Pillar to the magazine (aft)		50	Gun deck plank
22	Footwaling		51	Gun deck beam
23	Limber strakes		52	Quarterdeck beam
24	Garboard strakes		53	Quarterdeck plank
25	Keel		54	Quarterdeck berthing
			55	Rough-tree rail

C Internal hull

C1/4

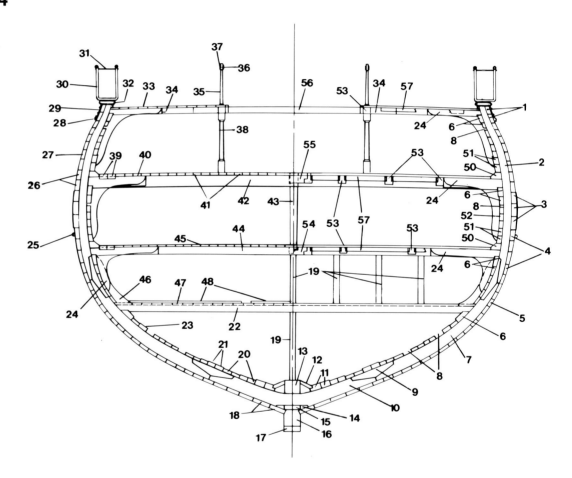

C1/5 Frame bend O aft of joint line from forward (port side 1/96 scale)

1 Extended timberhead
2 Planksheer
3 Berthing
4 Sheer strakes
5 Fore channel
6 Plank of the side
7 Thickstuff over the wales
8 Main wale
9 Diminishing planks and thickstuff
10 Batten over the copper
11 Plank of the bottom
12 Third futtock
13 Chock
14 Fore platform clamp
15 Lower futtock
16 Footwaling
17 Limber strakes
18 Garboard strakes
19 Keel
20 False keel
21 Rising wood
22 Cross chock
23 Keelson
24 Limber board
25 Fore mast step pillar
26 Block
27 Fore platform carling
28 Ledge
29 Fore mast step
30 Iron hoop
31 Fore platform plank
32 Fore platform beam
33 Fore platform standard
34 Quickwork
35 Clamp
36 Berth deck hanging knee
37 Berth deck carling
38 Berth deck beam
39 Berth deck ledge
40 Mast collar
41 Berth deck plank
42 Binding strakes
43 Berth deck waterway
44 Spirketting
45 Quickwork
46 Air space
47 Clamp
48 Gun deck hanging knee
49 Fore mast
50 Mast wedges
51 Gun deck beam
52 Lodging knee
53 Gun deck carling
54 Gun deck plank
55 Gun deck ledge
56 Binding strake
57 Gun deck waterway
58 Gun deck spirketting
59 Gun deck air space
60 Gun deck clamp
61 Forecastle dagger knee
62 Head ledge
63 Forecastle beam
64 Ledge
65 Hatch coaming
66 Hatch carling
67 Forecastle deck plank
68 Forecastle carling
69 Lodging knee
70 Binding strake
71 Forecastle waterway
72 Spirketting

C1/6 Frame bend V forward of joint line from aft (port side, 1/96 scale)

1 Rough-tree rail
2 Planksheer of the forecastle
3 Sheer strakes
4 Moulding
5 Plank of the side
6 Thickstuff over the wales
7 Main wale
8 Diminishing planks and thickstuff
9 Chock
10 Batten for copper
11 Plank of bottom
12 Second futtock
13 Garboard planks
14 Stem
15 Forefoot
16 Forward deadwood
17 Keelson
18 Limber strakes
19 Crutch
20 Footwaling
21 Berth deck clamp
22 Berth deck beam
23 Scuttle
24 Planked cover
25 Scuttle coaming
26 Berth deck coaming
27 Berth deck plank
28 Binding strakes
29 Waterway
30 Spirketting
31 Quickwork
32 Air space
33 Gun deck clamp
34 Gun deck beam
35 Ledge
36 Gun deck carling
37 Gun deck plank
38 Gun deck lodging knee
39 Gun deck hanging knee
40 Binding strake
41 Gun deck waterway
42 Gun deck spirketting
43 Quickwork
44 Forecastle hanging knee
45 Air space
46 Clamp
47 Lodging knee
48 Forecastle ledge
49 Forecasle beam
50 Forecastle carling
51 Forecastle deck plank
52 Binding strake
53 Forecastle waterway
54 Forecastle spirketting
55 Extended timberhead

C1/5

C1/6

55

C Internal hull

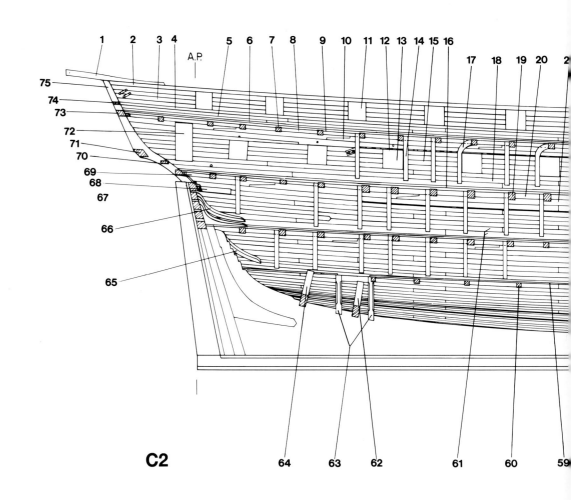

C2

22 23

24 25 26 27 28 29 30

31

32 33 34 35 36 37 38

39 40

F. P.

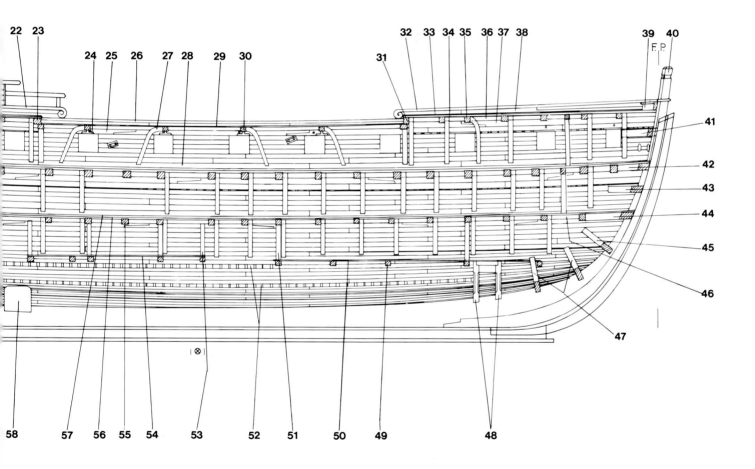

41

42

43

44

45

46

47

58 57 56 55 54 53 52 51 50 49 48

C Internal hull

C3   **HOLD – KENTLAGE (1/144 scale)**

1   Sternpost
2   Sternson
3   Bread room
4   Hanging knee
5   Bread room bulkhead
6   Light room bulkhead
7   Light room
8   Filling room bulkhead
9   Cant board
10   Magzine bulkhead
11   First tier casks
12   Wood pillar
13   Main mast
14   Well bulkhead
15   Cant board
16   Half pigs
17   Second tier pigs
18   First tier pigs in hold
19   Limber boards
20   Cant boards
21   Salt packing
22   Fore mast
23   Fore mast step
24   Wood pillar
25   Ceiling (pine)
26   Crutch
27   Stem
28   Apron
29   Stemson
30   Breasthook
31   Fore peak bulkhead
32   Fore hold bulkhead
33   Air space
34   Sand
35   Shingle
36   Keelson
37   Midships
38   Pillars
39   Shot locker
40   Well
41   Main mast step
42   After hold bulkhead
43   Sand
44   Plank of the bulkhead
45   Crutch
46   Mizzen mast step
47   Wood pillar
48   Crutch
49   Transom sleeper

C3

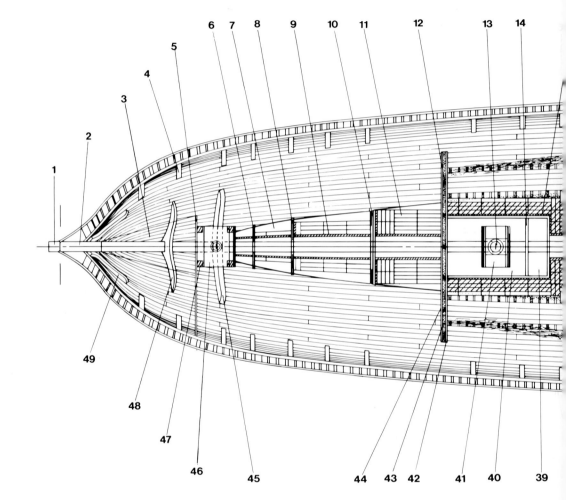

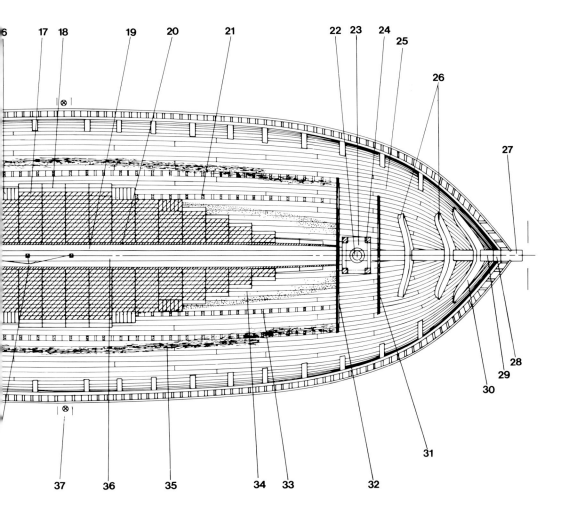

16   17 18   19   20   21   22 23   24   25   26

27

28

29

30

31

32

37   36   35   34 33

C Internal hull

C4 **HOLD – CASK STOWAGE (1/144 scale)**

1 Sternpost
2 Sternson
3 Transom sleeper
4 Crutch
5 Bread room
6 Tin lantern
7 Fixed window
8 Sliding panels to magazine
9 Copper plating to magazine
10 After platform bulkhead
11 Well
12 Main mast step
13 Well bulkhead
14 Wood chocks
15 Anchor stock
16 First tier casks
17 Wood filling strake
18 Hanging knee
19 Midship symbol
20 Fore hold bulkhead
21 Fore peak bulkhead
22 Breast hook
23 Stem
24 Apron
25 Stemson
26 Crutch
27 Fore mast
28 Fore mast step
29 Fore hold bulkhead
30 Second tier casks
31 Fore platform bulkhead
32 Wood pillar
33 Shot locker
34 Main mast
35 Sand
36 Magazine bulkhead
37 Second tier powder casks
38 First tier powder casks
39 Filling room planking
40 Filling room bulkhead
41 Planking to lightroom
42 Light room bulkhead
43 Scuttle to light room
44 Mizzen mast
45 Mizzen mast step
46 Bread room platform
47 Keelson

C4

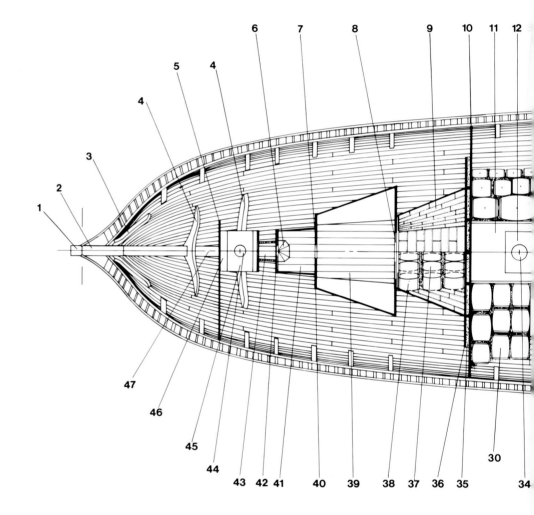

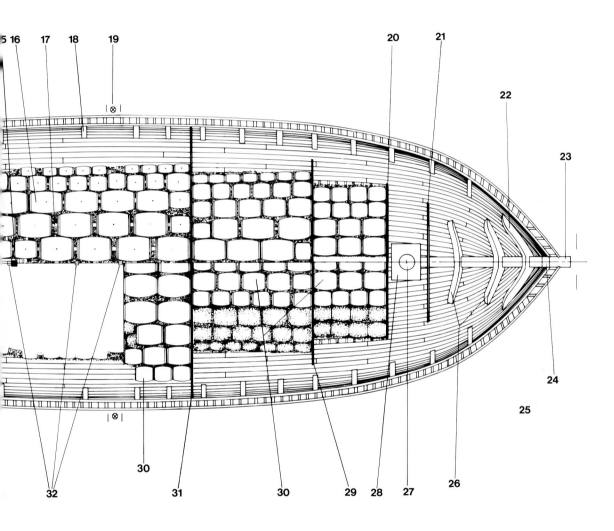

5 16   17   18   19   20   21   22   23

                                                                                                                    24

                                                                                              25

32   30   31   30   29 28 27   26

61

C Internal hull

C5 GALLEY STOVE (1/96 scale)

C5/1 Port elevation

1 Handgrips
2 Movable hood
3 Movable flap
4 Suspended arm (spit)
5 Spit wheels
6 Drip pan
7 Furnace
8 Ash pan
9 Oven door
10 Cock
11 Match bin
12 Railing
13 Steam valve
14 Covered pot
15 Chimney

C5/2 Plan view

1 Boiler lid
2 Covered pot lid
3 Chimney
4 Hood
5 Suspended arm (spit)
6 Spit
7 Drip pan
8 Lower spit wheel
9 Drive chain
10 Upper spit wheel
11 Railing
12 Covered pot lid
13 Boiler lid
14 Match bin
15 Steam valve

C5/3 Front elevation

1 Hand grip
2 Movable hood
3 Chimney
4 Upper spit wheel
5 Drive chain
6 Lower spit wheel
7 Match bin
8 Cocks
9 Railing
10 Movable flap

C5/2

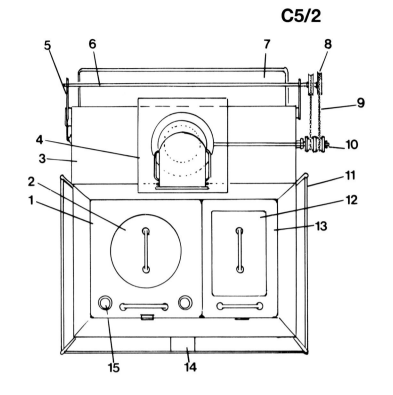

C5/1

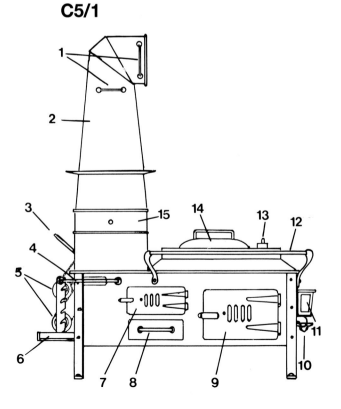

C5/3

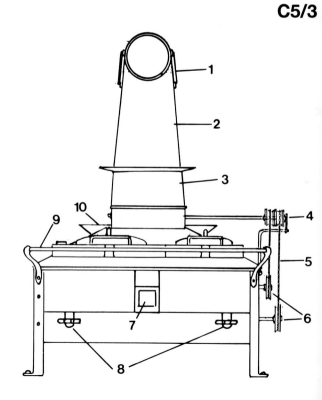

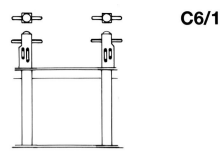

C6/1

C6/5

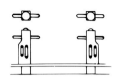

C6/5 Mizzen jeer bitts

C6 **BITTS (1/96 scale)**

C6/1 **Fore topsail sheet bitts (view from aft)**

1 Cross pin
2 Sheaves
3 Deck beam
4 Bitt pin

C6/3

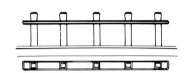

C6/3 **Gangway barricade at the waist (view from forward)**

1 Stanchions
2 Rail
3 Deck beam
4 Barricade – plan view
5 Belaying point (heads)

C6/6

C6/6 **Main jeer bitts (from aft)**

C6/2

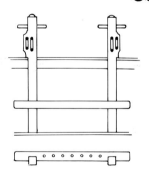

C6/2 **Fore jeer bitts (view from aft)**

1 Cross piece
2 Sheaves
3 Deck beam
4 Bitt pin
5 Foremast

C6/4

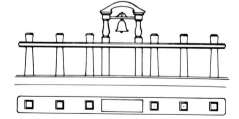

C6/4 **Barricade at forecastle and belfry**

1 Heads – belaying points
2 Rail
3 Stanchion
4 Deck beam
5 Belfry
6 Bell
7 Barricade plan view

C6/7

C6/7 **Main topsail sheet bitts (from forward)**

C Internal hull

C7 ORLOP DECK – CABLE TIER
(1/144 scale)

1   Sternson
2   Transom sleeper
3   Crutch
4   Platform to bread room
5   Mizzen mast
6   Scuttle to light room
7   Steward's store room
8   Marines' store room
9   After platform
10 Surgeon's store room
11 Cockpit
12 Ladderway
13 Shot locker
14 Cable
15 Cable tier
16 Third tier casks
17 Sailmaker's stores
18 Beam
19 Ledges
20 Carling
21 Boatswain's stores
22 Lodging knee
23 Foremast
24 Foremast step
25 Fish room
26 Breasthook
27 Stem
28 Apron
29 Stemson
30 Hanging knee
31 Gunroom bulkhead
32 Carling
33 Gunner's stores
34 Fixed planks
35 Movable planks
36 Horn lantern
37 Carpenter's stores
38 Ladderway
39 Paint locker
40 Lattice bulwark
41 Eyebolts
42 Movable planking of cable tier
43 Hatch grating
44 Anchor stock
45 Well
46 Scuttle to magazine
47 Lieutenant's store room
48 Slop room
49 Scuttle to filling room
50 Captain's storeroom
51 Mizzen mast
52 Planking to bread room
53 Inner post
54 Sternpost

C7

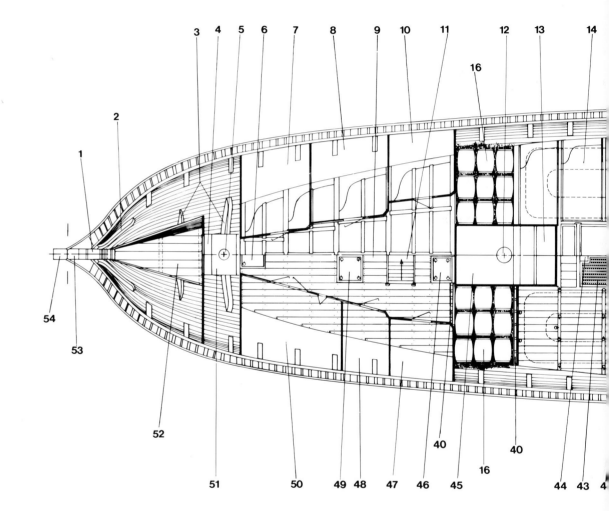

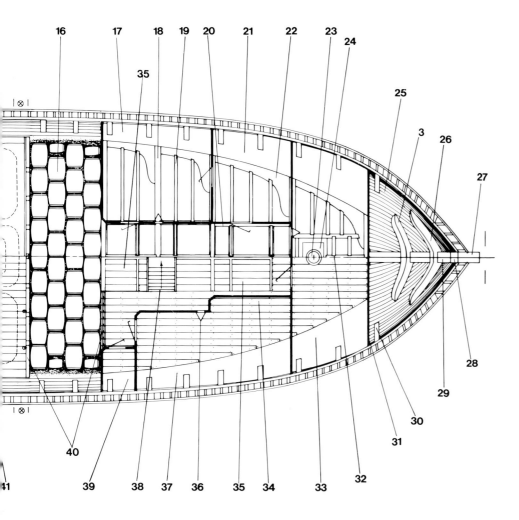

16 17 18 19 20 21 22 23 24

35

25

3 26

27

28

29

30

31

32

41 39 38 37 36 35 34 33

40

C8

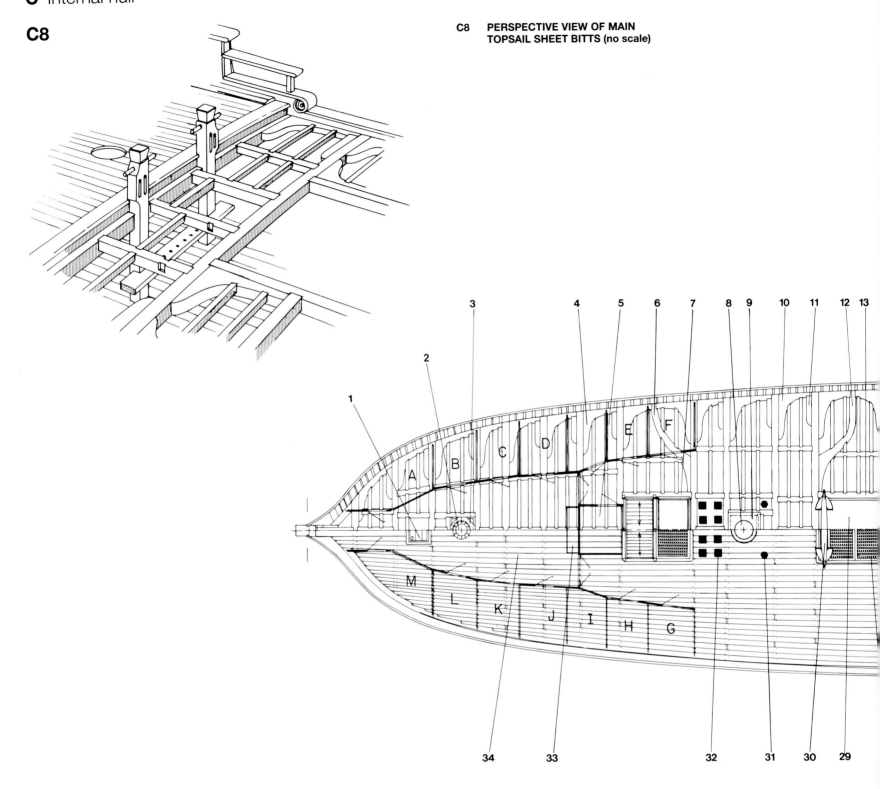

C9 **PLAN OF BERTH DECK (1/144 scale)**

1 Scuttle to bread room
2 Mizzen mast
3 Mizzen mast partners
4 Purser's store room
5 Steward's pantry
6 Spur beam
7 Hatch carling
8 Main mast
9 Main mast partners
10 Lodging knee
11 Hanging knee
12 Spur beam
13 Main hatch carling
14 Capstan bed
15 Ledge
16 Ladderway to gun deck
17 Fore hatch carling
18 Bitt pin
19 Carling
20 Foremast partners
21 Bitt pin
22 Deck hoop
23 Scuttle to fore peak
24 Foremast
25 Ladderway to orlop deck
26 Berth deck planking
27 Waterway
28 Grating
29 Main hatch
30 Spare anchor
31 Log pumps
32 Pump boxes
33 Wardroom pantry
34 Wardroom

Cabins
A Officers' bread room
B Lieutenant of marines
C Master
D Surgeon
E Captain's clerk
F Boatswain
G Carpenter
H Gunner
I Purser
J Captain of Marines
K First Lieutenant
L Second Lieutenant
M Vegetable stores

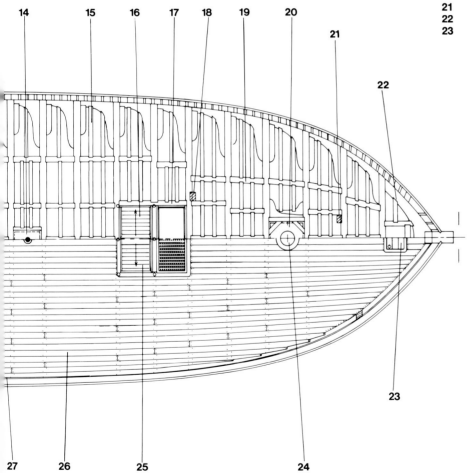

C9

C Internal hull

C10   PLAN OF THE GUN DECK (1/144 scale)

1   Iron knee
2   Tiller sweep
3   Lobby
4   Mizzen mast
5   Hatch coaming
6   Capstan bed
7   Ladderway to berth deck
8   Pillar
9   Bitt pin
10 Mainmast
11 Mainmast wedges
12 Log pumps
13 Spur beam
14 Main hatch carling
15 Capstan partner
16 Gun deck beam
17 Lodging knee
18 Hanging knee
19 Fore hatch coaming
20 Ledge
21 Carling
22 Scuttle to berth deck
23 Scupper
24 Pump
25 Manger
26 Roller
27 Bowsprit bitt
28 Fore riding bits
29 Fore mast partners
30 Fore mast
31 Fore mast coat
32 Bearing (water trough under stove)
33 Galley stove
34 Main cable bitts
35 Fore hatch
36 Ladderway below deck
37 Fore hatch coaming
38 Jeer capstan
39 Ringbolts
40 Main hatch coaming
41 Main hatch grating
42 Pillar to gangboard
43 Main topsail sheet bitt
44 Main mast coat
45 Chain pumps
46 Pump crank
47 Waterway
48 Trundlehead (capstan)
49 Hatch coaming
50 Hatch grating
51 Ladderway to quarterdeck
52 Tiller rope pipe
53 Movable partition
54 Captain's bed place
55 Great cabin
56 12pdr

C10

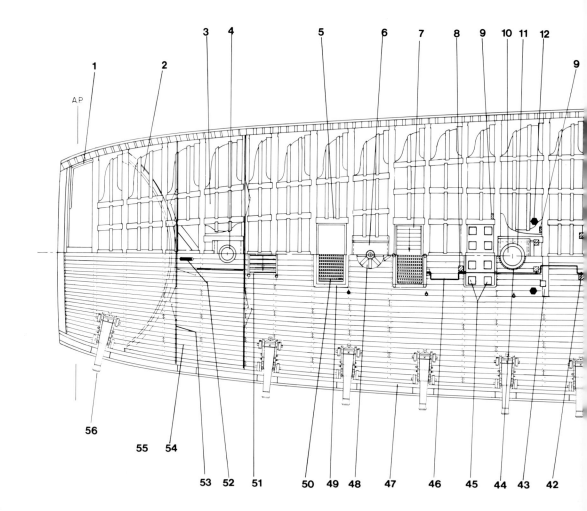

14 15 16 17 18 19 20 21

22

23

FP

24

25

26

27

28

39 38 37 36 35 34 33 32 31 30 29

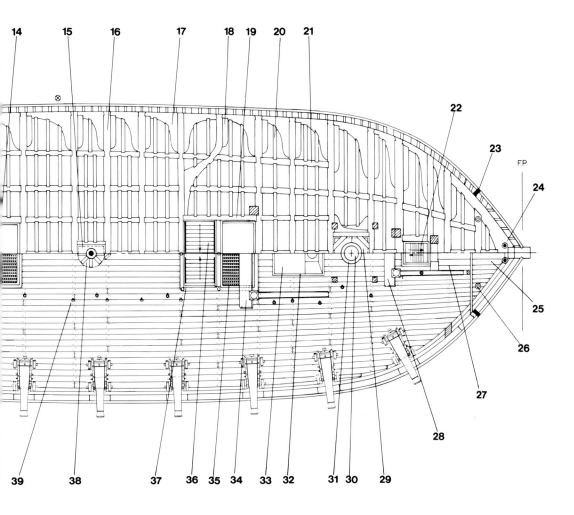

C11

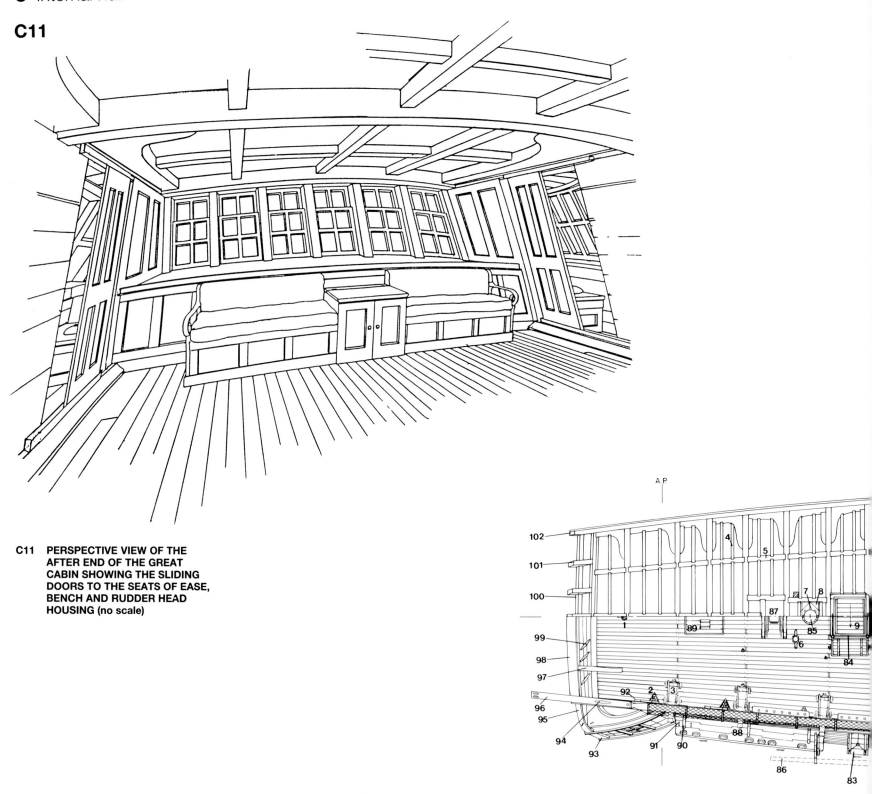

**C11   PERSPECTIVE VIEW OF THE
AFTER END OF THE GREAT
CABIN SHOWING THE SLIDING
DOORS TO THE SEATS OF EASE,
BENCH AND RUDDER HEAD
HOUSING (no scale)**

C12	**QUARTERDECK – WAIST – FORECASTLE (framing and deck arrangement, 1/144 scale)**	23	Barricade	50	Breasthood pin rail	77	Ringbolt for train trackle
		24	Ladder to gun deck	51	Cap rail	78	Pin rail (quarterdeck)
		25	Hanging knee (gangway)	52	Eyebolt bowsprit shroud	79	Capstan bar
1	Sheet block	26	Main hatch grating	53	Eyebolt for jib guy	80	Eyebolt plates
2	Shot rack	27	Lodging knee	54	Cathead	81	Lightning rod chain (stowed flaked)
3	6pdr	28	Pillar (gun deck)	55	Anchor block	82	Hammock netting
4	Ledge (quarterdeck)	29	Jeer capstan (gun deck)	56	Fore mast cleat	83	12pdr port lid
5	Carling (quarterdeck)	30	Jeer capstan bar (gun deck)	57	Bill block	84	Companionway railing
6	Mizzen topsail sheet bitt	31	Half beam	58	Studdingsail boom bracket	85	Mizzen mast
7	Mast cleats (mizzen)	32	Carling (gangway)	59	Bracket for fish davit	86	Studdingsail boom
8	Mizzen mast partners	33	Skid beam	60	Timberhead	87	Twelve-spoke wheel (helm)
9	Companionway	34	Ladderway (fore hatch gun deck)	61	Eyebolt to secure anchor	88	Mizzen channel
10	Small arms chests (four on quarterdeck)	35	Grating (fore hatch gun deck)	62	Position of stowed anchor	89	Hen coop
11	Hatch	36	After riding bitts	63	Fore channel	90	Hammock crane
12	Capstan spindle	37	Standard (gun deck)	64	Railing bracket	91	Eyebolt for backstays
13	Capstan bed	38	Belfry, forecastle	65	Chesstree	92	Range cleat
14	Capstan stop	39	Barricade	66	Jeer capstan stop	93	Quarter gallery
15	Quarterdeck planking	40	Barricade knee	67	Plank of the side	94	Cleat (boat fall)
16	Quarterdeck beam	41	Hood (galley stove, gun deck)	68	Gangboards	95	Quarter board
17	Main jeer bitts	42	Fore jeer bitts	69	Gangway railing	96	Boat davit
18	Main mast partners	43	Fore topsail sheet fitts	70	Scuppers	97	Transom knee
19	Main mast	44	Steam hatch	71	Skids	98	Taffrail
20	Main topsail sheet bitts	45	Forecastle deck planking	72	Boarding steps	99	Cleat
21	Scuttle to main topsail sheet bitts	46	Roller socket	73	Boarding rope	100	Necking transom
22	Gangway hatch	47	Bowsprit	74	Main mast cleat	101	Stern knee
		48	Iron strap	75	Channel knee	102	Side timber
		49	Rough-tree rail	76	Main channel		

C12

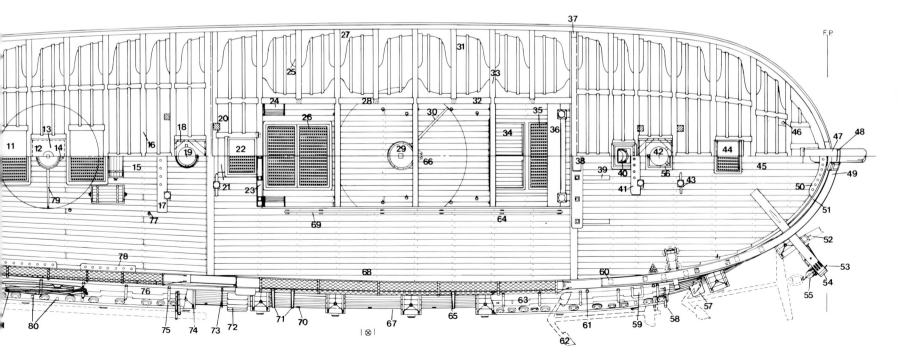

C13 INBOARD PROFILE – DECK DETAILS (no scale)

1 Stern davit
2 Stern lantern
3 Laniard (hammock nettings)
4 Kevel block
5 Hammock crane (iron)
6 Hen coop
7 Hammock netting
8 6pdr
9 Shot rack
10 Helm
11 Mizzen topsail sheet bitts
12 Mizzen mast
13 Mast cleats
14 Companionway rail
15 Small arms chest (five on quarterdeck)
16 Capstan (drumhead)
17 Main jeer bitts

18 Mainmast
19 Mainmast cleats
20 Main topsail sheet bitts
21 Barricade
22 Gangboard stanchion (iron)
23 Gangboard rail (wood)
24 Longboat stowed on skid beams
25 Yawl
26 Gangboard carling
27 Standards to belfry and barricade
28 Removable hood to the galley stove
29 Fore jeer bitts
30 Foremast cleats
31 Foremast
32 Fore topsail sheet bitts
33 Eyebolts in deck
34 Cat block
35 Cleat (stopper rope)
36 Splash board
37 Iron strap

Gun deck
38 Pump
39 Pump brake block
40 Roller
41 Manger
42 Bowsprit bitts
43 Fore riding bitts
44 12pdr
45 Fire bucket
46 Galley stove
47 Bearers under stove
48 Main jeer bits
49 Fore hatchway
50 Pillar to the gangway
51 Jeer capstan
52 Main hatch
53 Main topsail sheet bitts
54 Ladderway to gangway
55 Log pump
56 Mast wedges

57 Pump crank standard
58 Hood
59 Pump dale outlets
60 Pump crank
61 Capstan spindle
62 Ventilation hatch
63 Companionway ladder
64 Captain's bedplace (starboard)
65 Wheel rope (pipe and mast inboard of bedplace; shown for continuity)
66 Pantry
67 Captain's dining table and chairs
68 Cleat (rudder preventer rope)
69 Sliding door to quarter gallery
70 Quarter gallery
71 Bench
72 Double hung stern window
73 Curtain valances

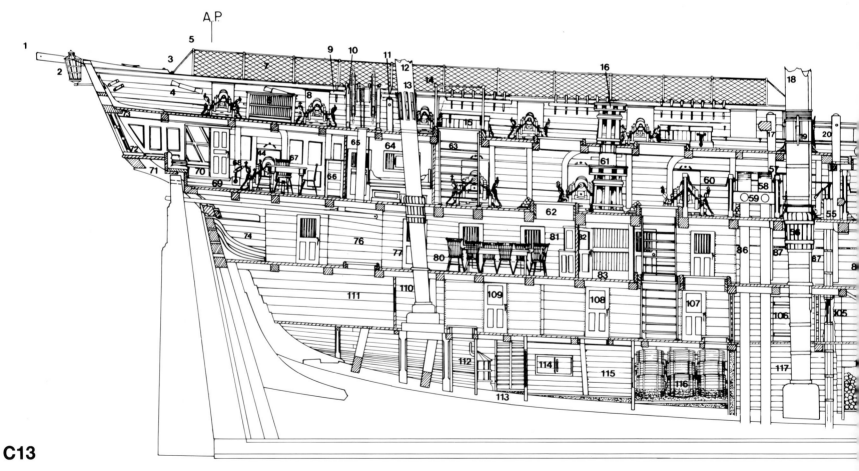

C13

Berth deck		Orlop – cable tier		Hold	
74	Ladies' hole	**95**	Water intake pipe through hawse piece	**112**	Lantern vent
75	Officers' bread room			**113**	Light room
76	Wardroom	**96**	Fore peak	**114**	Sliding panel to wings
77	Lieutenant of marines	**97**	Gunner's store room	**115**	Filling room
78	Master	**98**	Tin lantern	**116**	Powder magazine
79	Surgeon	**99**	Door to gunroom	**117**	Well
80	Painted fan-back chairs and table	**100**	Boatswain's stores	**118**	Cut-away of shot locker
81	Pantry	**101**	Sailmaker's stores	**119**	Wood chocks
82	Door to wardroom	**102**	Fore platform (orlop deck)	**120**	Main hold
83	Captain's pantry	**103**	Cable tier	**121**	Fore hold
84	Captain's clerk	**104**	16in cable		
85	Boatswain	**105**	Cut-away of pump well		
86	Chain pump box	**106**	Door to the pump room		
87	Iron hoops	**107**	Surgeon's store room		
88	Berth deck	**108**	Marines' store room		
89	Stowed sheet anchor	**109**	Steward's store room		
90	Capstan spindle (jeer)	**110**	Wings		
91	Staggered hammock locations (crew)	**111**	Bread room		
92	Mast coat (wood)				
93	Lead water pipe)				
94	Spigot				

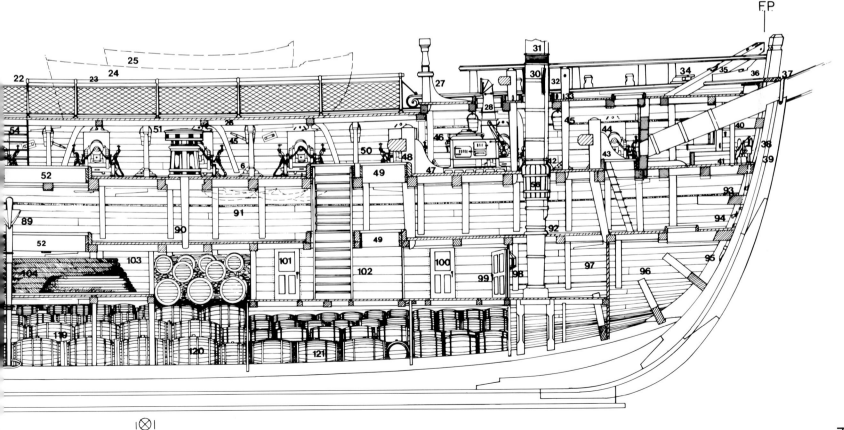

D Helm

D1	**WHEEL – DOUBLE (1/24 scale)**		**D2**	**RUDDER (1/48 scale)**

D1/1 View from aft

D1/2 Athwartship view (one wheel and
stanchion omitted for clarity)

D1/3 Stanchion detail

1	Hub (brass)
2	Knave
3	Rim (brass)
4	Spoke pin
5	Spoke
6	King pin
7	Felloe
8	Barrel
9	Wheel
10	Washer
11	Spindle
12	Stanchion
13	Iron bracket
14	Pad

D2/1 Rudder from starboard

D2/2 Sections of rudder

D2/3 Rudder from aft

D2/4 Rudder fixings and tiller

1	Main piece oak
2	Bearding piece elm
3	Oak piece
4	Back piece pine
5	Sole pine
6	Rabbet
7	Section through head
8	Section between hances
9	Section through rudder blade
10	Spare tiller hole
11	Tiller arm hole
12	Eyebolt
13	Ringbolt
14	Back piece
15	Sole
16	Head hoops
17	Upper hance
18	Upper pintle strap
19	Lower hance
20	Pintle strap
21	Forelock of tiller arm
22	Tiller arm
23	Wing transom
24	Inner post
25	Gudgeon strap
26	Pintle
27	Rabbet of the post
28	Keel
29	False keel
30	Bearding

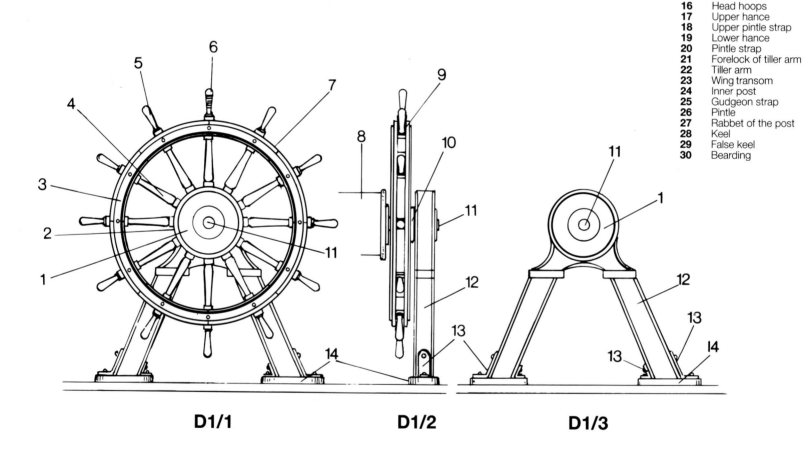

D1/1 **D1/2** **D1/3**

D2/1

D2/2

D2/3

D2/4

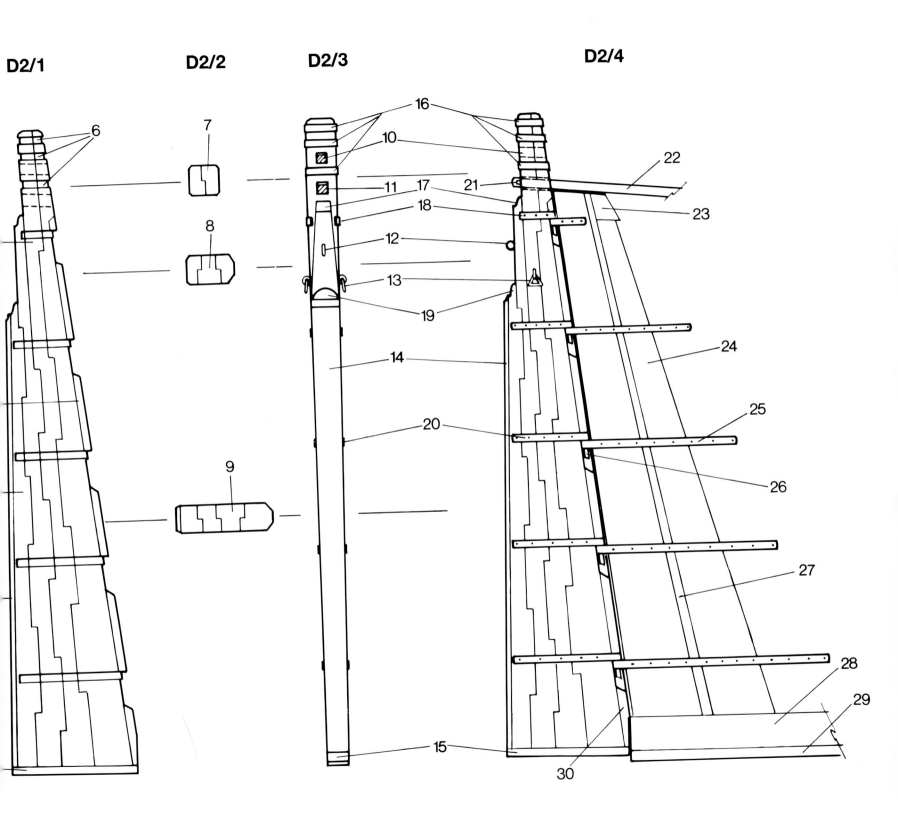

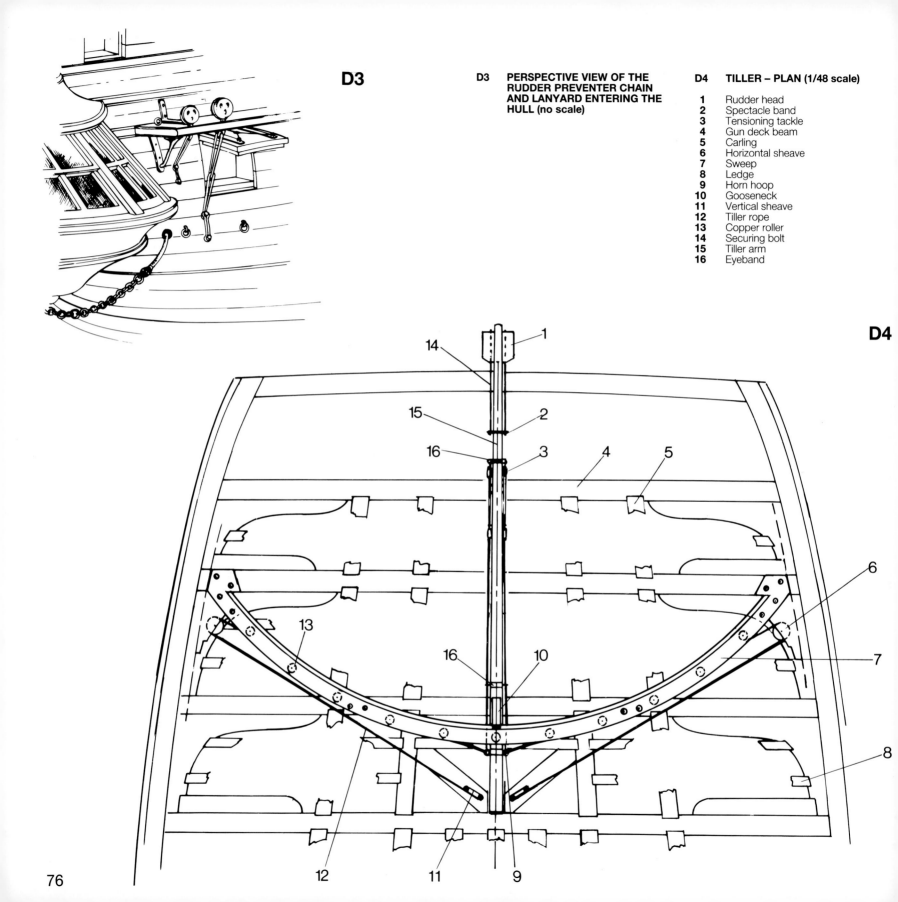

D3

D3 PERSPECTIVE VIEW OF THE
RUDDER PREVENTER CHAIN
AND LANYARD ENTERING THE
HULL (no scale)

D4 TILLER – PLAN (1/48 scale)

1 Rudder head
2 Spectacle band
3 Tensioning tackle
4 Gun deck beam
5 Carling
6 Horizontal sheave
7 Sweep
8 Ledge
9 Horn hoop
10 Gooseneck
11 Vertical sheave
12 Tiller rope
13 Copper roller
14 Securing bolt
15 Tiller arm
16 Eyeband

D4

E1 **12PDR 7FT CARRIAGE GUN (1/24 scale)**

E1/1 Plan view

E1/2 Rear elevation

E1/3 Side elevation

E1/4 Fore elevation

E1/5 Inboard elevation

1	Gun tackle eyebolt
2	Hind truck
3	Hind axletree
4	Linch pin
5	Bracket bolt
6	Gun tackle loop
7	Breeching eyebolt
8	Capsquare eyebolt
9	Capsquare
10	Trunnion
11	Capsquare joint bolt
12	Apron
13	Fore axletree
14	Fore truck
15	Pan
16	Loop
17	Button
18	Base ring
19	Bracket
20	Bolster
21	Quoin
22	Train tackle eyebolt
23	Stool bed
24	Chamber
25	First reinforce ring
26	Second reinforce ring and moulding
27	Capsquare key chain
28	Bore
29	Muzzle astragal
30	Muzzle thickening
31	Moulding
32	Transom bolt
33	Bed bolt
34	Transom
35	Staples
36	Axletree stay

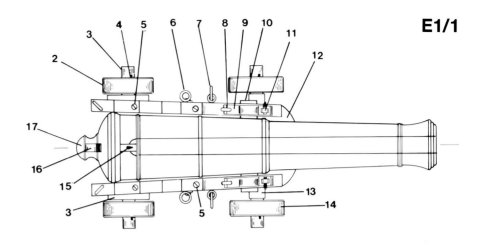

E1/1

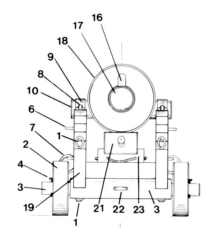

E1/2

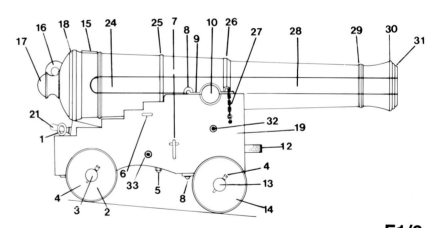

E1/3

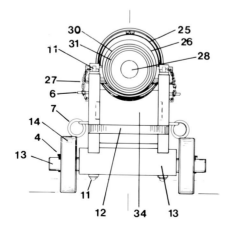

E1/4

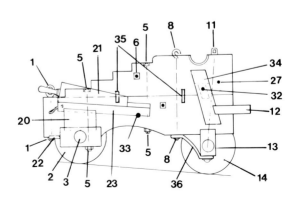

E1/5

E Armament

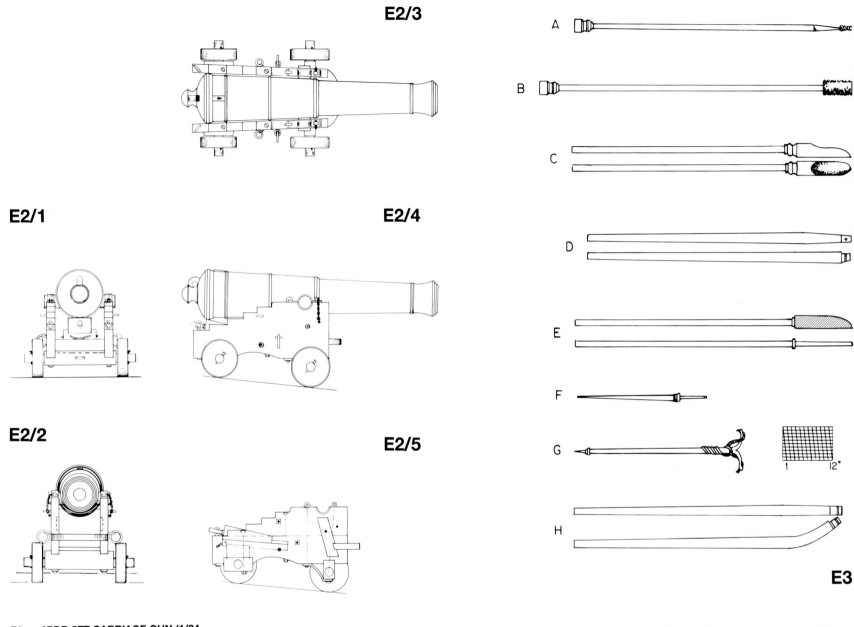

E2/3

E2/1

E2/4

E2/2

E2/5

A

B

C

D

E

F

G

H

E3

E2	6PDR 5FT CARRIAGE GUN (1/24 scale)
E2/1	Rear elevation
E2/2	Front elevation
E2/3	Plan view
E2/4	Side elevation
E2/5	Inboard elevation

E3	GUN EQUIPMENT (1/24 scale)
A	Wad hook
B	Sponge
C	Ladle (side and plan view)
D	Straight hand spike (side and plan view)
E	Reamer (side and plan view)
F	Port-fire stock
G	Lint stock
H	Crooked hand spike (side and plan view)

E4 **GUN TACKLES (gun deck port side profile, seventh 12pdr from forward, 1/24 scale)**

1	Gangboard	15	Port lid lining
2	Skid beam	16	12pdr (run out)
3	Ledge	17	Through hull bolts
4	Lantern	18	Breeching bolt
5	Port tackle cleat	19	Gun tackle ringbolt
6	Gun tackle implements	20	Shot rack
7	Fire bucket	21	Sponge tub
8	Gun port tackle	22	Crooked hand spike
9	Port laniard	23	Gun deck
10	Laniard ring	24	12pdr gun carriage
11	Gun port lid	25	Gun tackle
12	Eyebolt	26	Train tackle
13	Gun port lid strap	27	Pillar
14	Port hinge	28	Ringbolt (train tackle)
		29	Breeching rope
		30	Securing eyebolt

E4

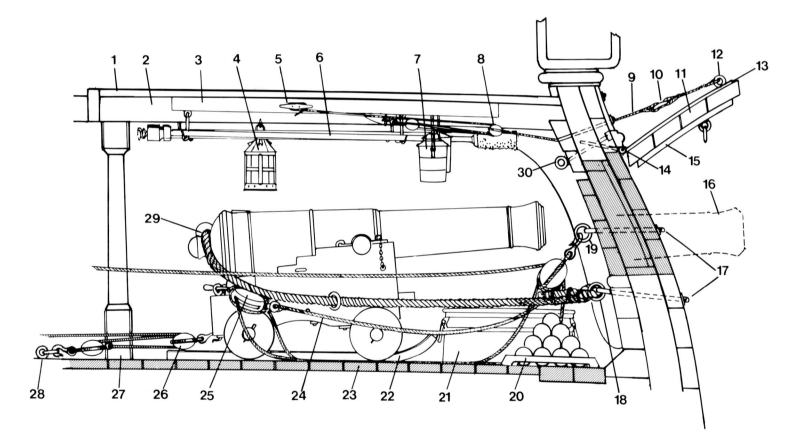

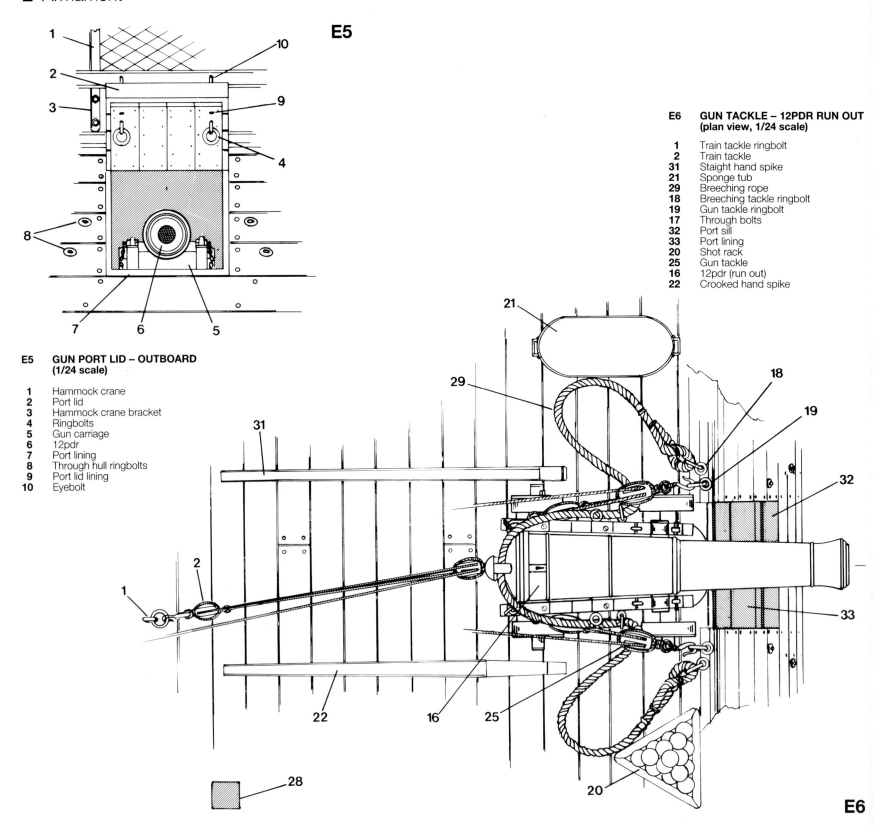

E5

E5   GUN PORT LID – OUTBOARD
(1/24 scale)

1 Hammock crane
2 Port lid
3 Hammock crane bracket
4 Ringbolts
5 Gun carriage
6 12pdr
7 Port lining
8 Through hull ringbolts
9 Port lid lining
10 Eyebolt

E6   GUN TACKLE – 12PDR RUN OUT
(plan view, 1/24 scale)

1 Train tackle ringbolt
2 Train tackle
31 Staight hand spike
21 Sponge tub
29 Breeching rope
18 Breeching tackle ringbolt
19 Gun tackle ringbolt
17 Through bolts
32 Port sill
33 Port lining
20 Shot rack
25 Gun tackle
16 12pdr (run out)
22 Crooked hand spike

E6

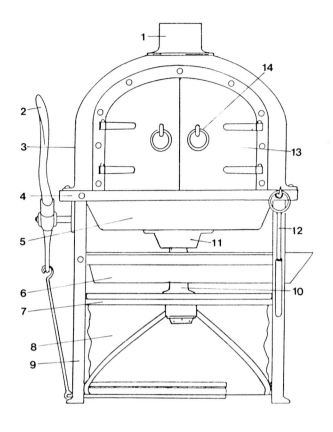

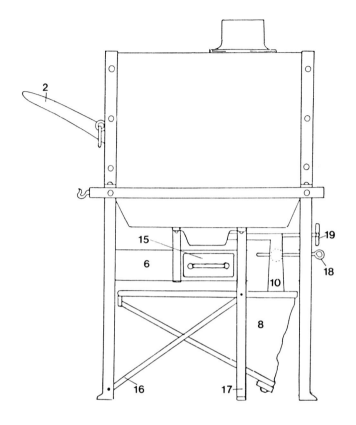

E7   ARMOURER'S FORGE (no scale)

E7/1   View from forward

E7/2   Side view

1	Chimney
2	Rocker staff
3	Furnace
4	Frame
5	Forge
6	Cast iron pan-shot to charge [fill] furnace.
7	Iron frame
8	Bellows
9	Iron legs
10	Air pipe
11	Tuyere (grate)
12	Ring shovel
13	Door
14	Ringbolt
15	Ash pan
16	Cross brace
17	Standard
18	Flow reglator
19	Grate adjustment

Original   description

An Armorer's Forge with Cast Iron bottom & deep Wroᵗ Iron Rim round the edge of do- 4 Square Wroᵗ Iron feet with a Cross Brace to Support the forge, a strong Wroᵗ Iron frame for the Bellows with 2 Standards & 3 Strong Cross and shifting Braces & Nuts with Cradle and Rock Staff. A Cast Iron Pan fixed in a wrought Iron frame under the forge to receive the Shott to Charge the Furnace, Cast Iron Furnace with door & 2 Ring Bolts – Strong Iron Chain with 2 Hooks for fixing to the forge. Iron Ring Shovel for taking out the Shott when hot, with 1 Pair Bellows For the Same

F External hull

F1 **HULL PLANKING (1/144 scale)**

F1/1 **Sheer**

F1/2 **Half-breadth**

1 Garboard strake
2 Sternpost
3 Lower counter
4 Upper counter
5 Quarterdeck transom
6 Doorway to quarter gallery
7 6pdr port (quarterdeck)
8 12pdr port (gun deck)
9 Port lining
10 Berthing
11 Quarterdeck planksheer
12 Sheer strakes
13 Forecastle planksheer
14 Thickstuff
15 Hawse holes
16 Main wale
17 Diminishing planks
18 Plank of the bottom
19 Keel
20 Keel scarf
21 False keel scarf
22 Stem
23 Rudder port
24 Plank of the lower counter
25 Filling half timbers
26 Upper counter and support
27 Stern knees
28 Stern side timber
29 Quarterdeck transom and support for quarter gallery

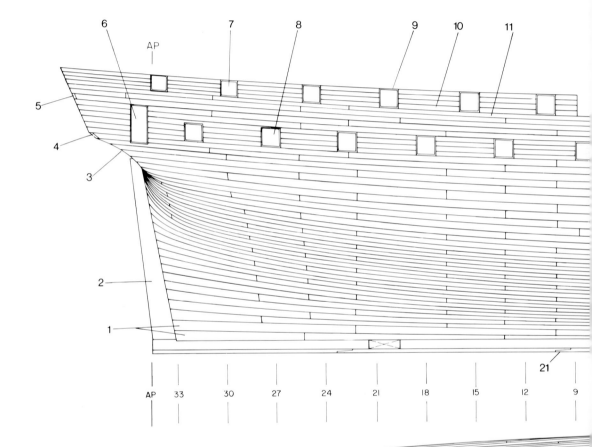

F1/1

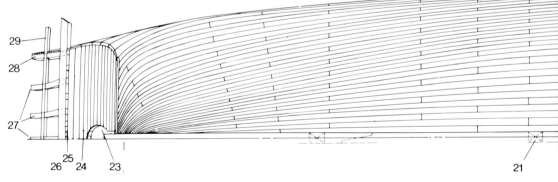

F1/2

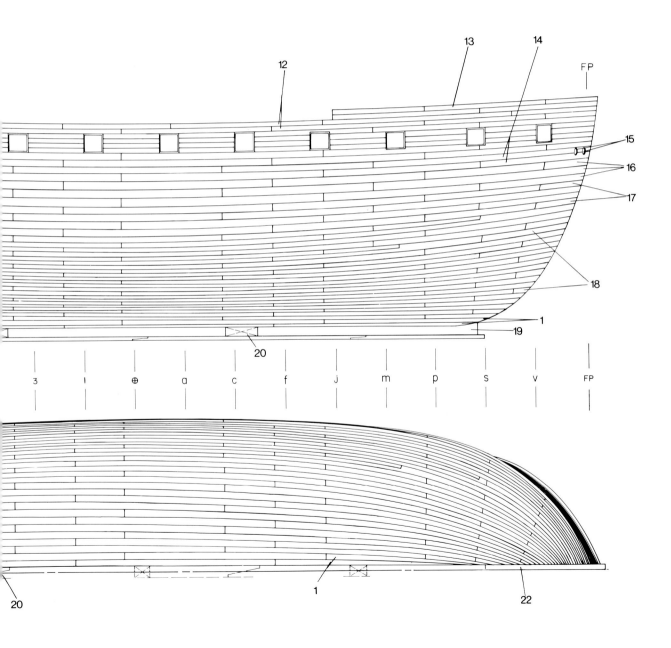

12

13

14

FP

15

16

17

18

1

19

20

3   I   ⊕   a   c   f   j   m   p   s   v   FP

20

1

22

F External hull

F2 EXTERNAL DETAILS AND SHEATHING (1/144 scale)

F2/1 Sheer

F2/2 Half-breadth

1 Underside of the keel
2 Underside rudder blade
3 Copper staples
4 Gudgeon strap
5 Pintle strap
6 Lower hance
7 Rudder preventer bolt
8 Upper hance
9 End of tiller arm
10 Quarter board
11 Boat davit
12 Double hung window
13 Mizzen chain plates
14 Chain preventer ringbolt
15 Mizzen mast
16 Wooden batten
17 Moulding
18 Rough-tree rail
19 Main chain plate
20 Leaded scupper hole
21 Main mast
22 Boarding steps
23 Gangboard railing
24 Fenders
25 Fastening of the planks
26 Chesstree
27 Fore chains
28 Fore mast
29 Anchor block
30 Cathead
31 Bollard timber (knighthead)
32 Splash board
33 Bowsprit
34 Bolster
35 Scupper to the manger
36 Coppering of the stem
37 False keel
38 Keel
39 Sternpost coppering
40 False keel
41 Copper of the stem

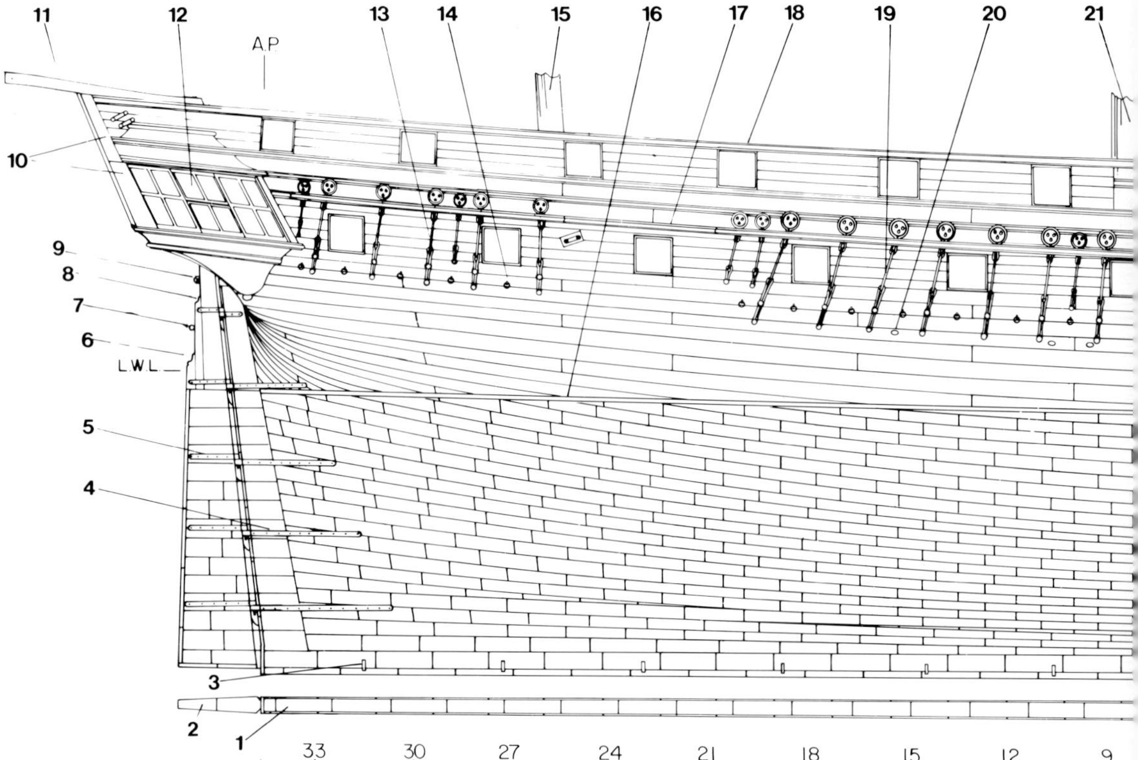

F2/1

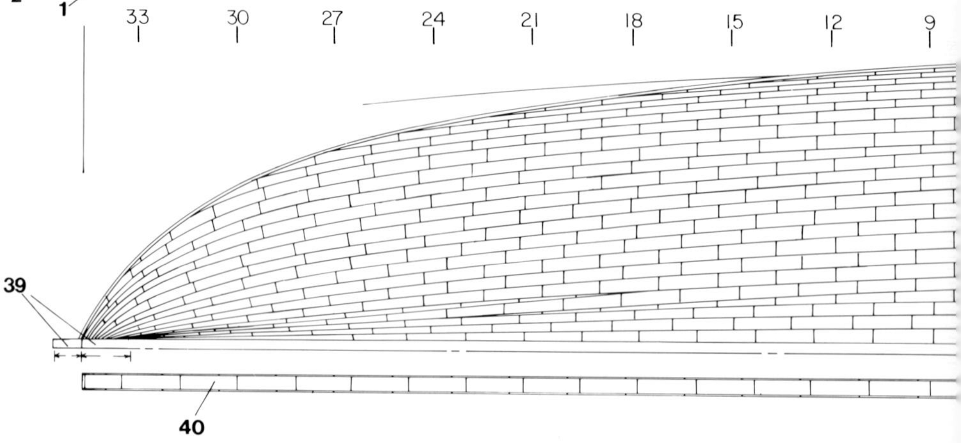

F2/2

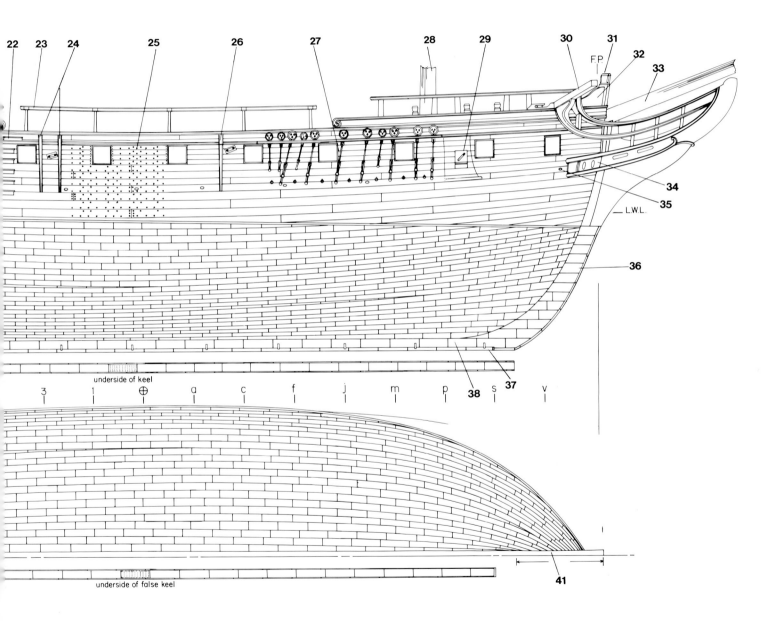

22 23 24 25 26 27 28 29 30 31 32 33

F.P.

34

35

L.W.L.

36

underside of keel

3   1   ⊕   a   c   f   j   m   p   s   v

38   37

41

underside of false keel

F External hull

F3 **EXTERIOR HULL COMPLETED (no scale)**

1	Preventer chain ringbolt	**7**	Shingles (hollow top)	
2	Rudder chain laniard	**8**	Laniard (hammock netting)	
3	Boat davit	**9**	Iron stanchion	
4	Stern lantern	**10**	Hammock netting	
5	Taffrail	**11**	Quarterdeck gun port	
6	Fixed block (main and preventer brace)	**12**	Iron bracket	
		13	Port lid laniard	
		14	Studdingsail boom bracket	
		15	Socket for swing boom	

16	Paint line (mizzen mast)
17	Sheave for main sheet
18	Swivel eyebolt for main sheet (standing end)
19	Gun port lid
20	Chain plate preventer ringbolt
21	Iron knee
22	Paint line for mainmast
23	Socket for main swing boom

24	Boarding rope
25	Iron stanchion (gangway–waist)
26	Wooden railing
27	Eyebolt
28	Belfry
29	Stanchion head
30	Knee
31	Paint line (foremast)
32	Socket – fore swing boom

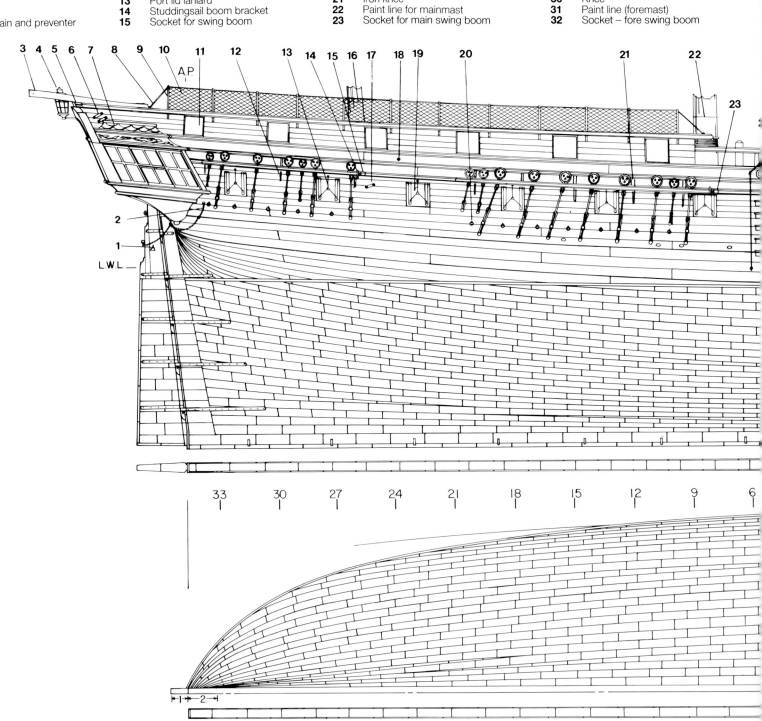

F3

33	Anchor lining	**42**	Bowsprit
34	Billboard	**43**	Figurehead
35	Bill block	**44**	Bobstay holes
36	Eyebolt (bumpkin shroud)	**45**	Ringbolt (bumpkin shrouds)
37	Cathead	**46**	Gammoning slots
38	Gammoning cleats	**47**	Wash cant
39	Iron stanchion		
40	Fairlead		
41	Iron railing		

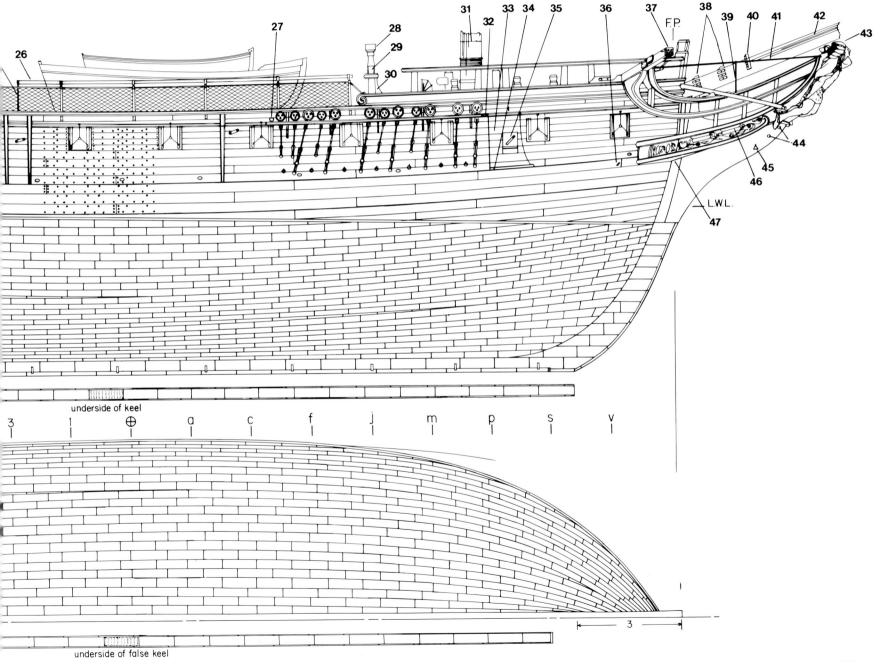

underside of keel

underside of false keel

F External hull

1   Tenon for cap
2   Bowsprit
3   Figurehead
4   Rough-tree rail
5   Headrails
6   Splash board
7   Boomkin
8   Timberhead
9   Cathead
10 6pdr port opening
11 Bridle port
12 Fore channel
13 Anchor block
14 12pdr
15 Scupper to the manger
16 Eyebolt for bumpkin shroud
17 Wash cant
18 Copper of the bottom
19 Pump intake

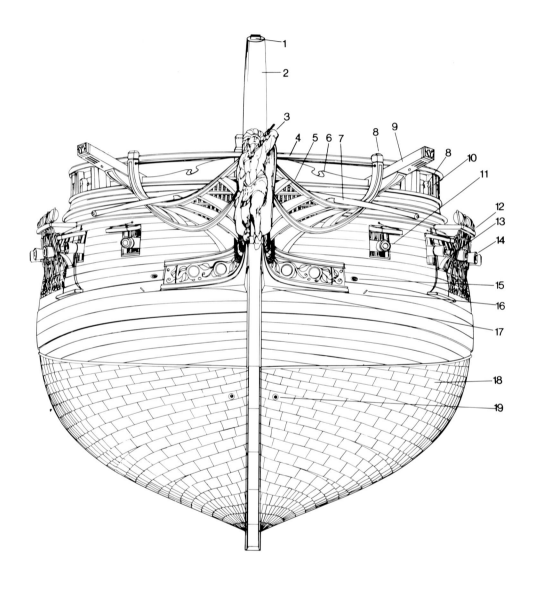

F5   **FLAGS AND PENNANTS (1/48 scale)**

F5/1   Ensign (16ft x 9ft 6in)

F5/2   Jack (size of the ensign's canton)

F5/3   Commodore's broad pennant (12ft x 5ft)

F5/4   Commissioning pennant (40ft x 15¹⁄₁₆in)

F5/1

F5/2

F5/3

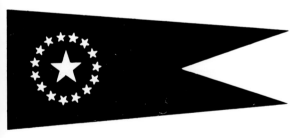

F5/4

89

G Anchors and cables

G1

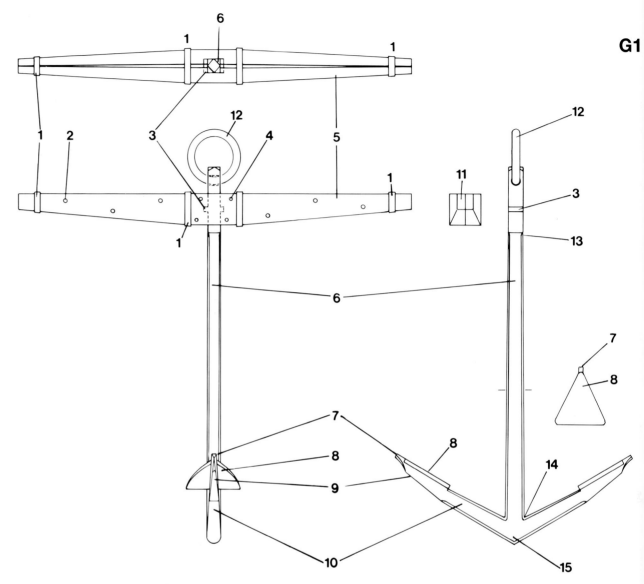

G2

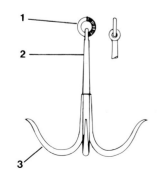

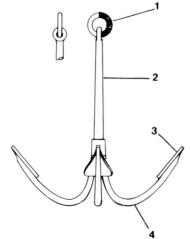

G3

G4

G4   10cwt STREAM ANCHOR (1/96 scale)

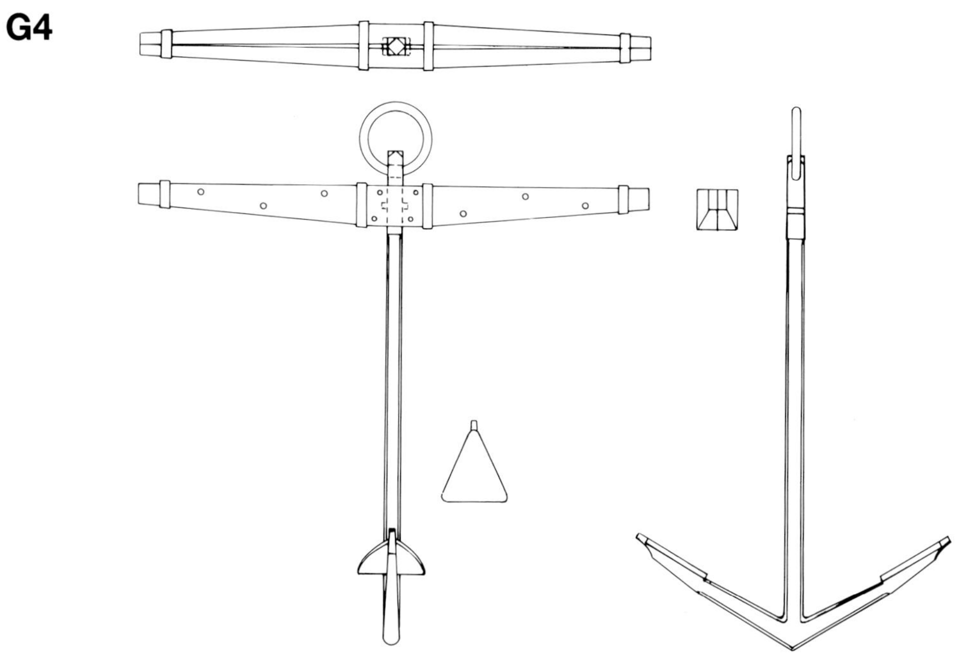

G4

G5   5cwt KEDGE ANCHOR (1/24 scale)

1   Stop
2   Stock
3   Forelock and chain
4   Ring
5   Palm
6   Eye
7   Shank

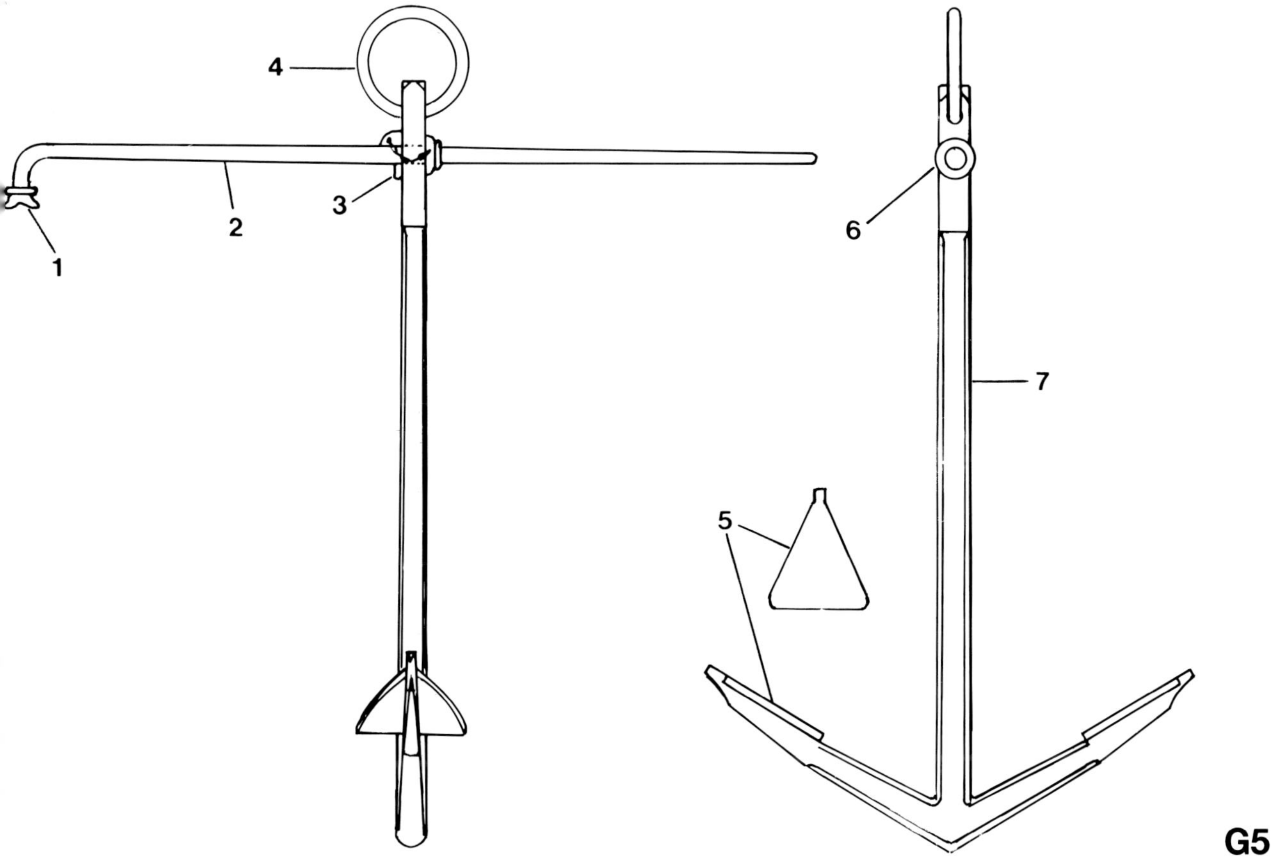

G5

G Anchors and cables

G6 ANCHOR STOWAGE (1/96 scale)

G6/1 Plan view (starboard side)

1   Eyebolt (fish davit guy)
2   Hammock netting
3   Lashing
4   Sheer rail
5   Rough-tree rail
6   Topping lift
7   Timberhead
8   6pdr
9   Eyebolt (deck)
10 Port opening
11 Cathead
12 Cleat
13 Stopper rope (served whole length)
14 Anchor cable
15 Stoper knot
16 Cat block rope
17 Bower No 2
18 Port lid
19 Bill block
20 Studdingsail boom bracket
21 Fish davit
22 Fore channel
23 Bower No 4

G6/1

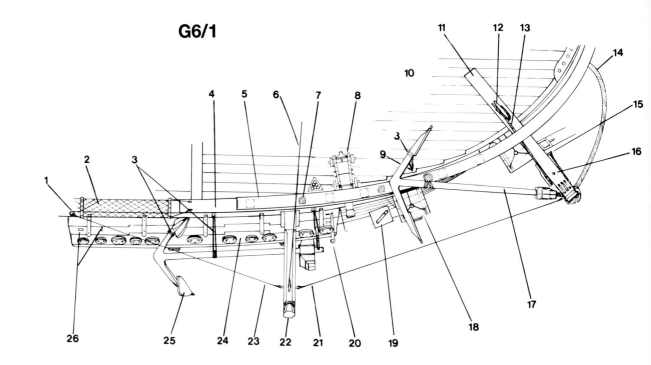

G6/2 Profile (starboard side)

1   Eyebolt (fish davit guy)
2   Hammock netting
3   Barricade
4   Belfry
5   Lashing
6   After guy
7   Davit block
8   Fish davit
9   Topping lift
10 Fore mast
11 6pdr
12 Timberhead
13 Fore guy
14 Snatch block
15 Bower No 2
16 Stopper
17 Cat fall
18 Anchor cable
19 Scupper (manger)
20 Eyebolt
21 Port lid
22 Bill block
23 Fore channel
24 Bower No 4
25 Deck scupper

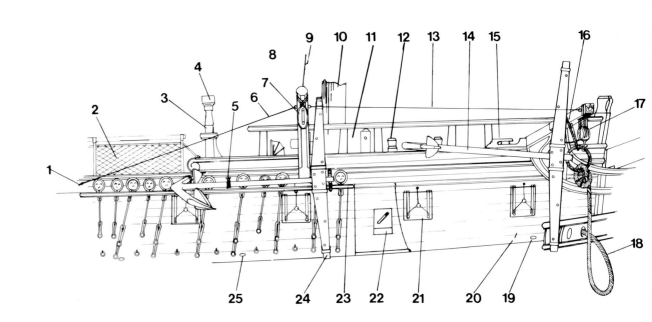

G6/2

G7   FISH DAVIT (1/48 scale)

G7/1   Plan view

1   Eyebolts
2   Octagonal section
3   Square
4   Heel (bevelled)

G7/2   Profile

1   Square section
2   Octagonal
3   Eyebolts
4   Davit block
5   Anchor hook
6   Fish tackle
7   Channel
8   Bed block

G8   VIOL BLOCK IN USE FOR WEIGHING ANCHOR (no scale)

1   After capstan
2   Main mast
3   Strap
4   Viol block (24in)
5   Viol messenger
6   Compressor
7   Nipper
8   Jeer capstan
9   Anchor cable
10   Fore mast
11   Roller
12   Hawse hole
13   Manger
14   Main hatch

G7/1

G7/2

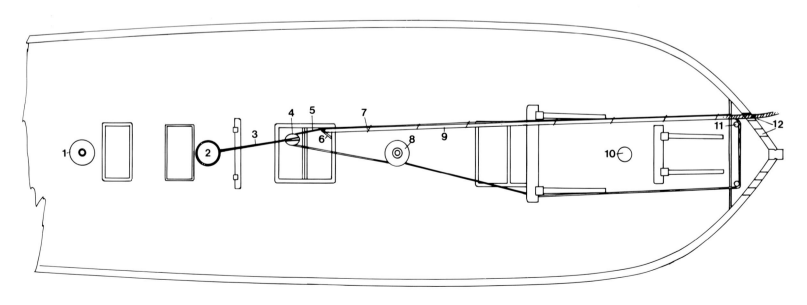

G8

93

G Anchors and cables

G9 CAPSTAN – CONSTRUCTION (1/24 scale)

G9/1 Structural section

G9/2 Side elevation

G9/3 Sections

G9/4 Capstan bars

1	Cap
2	Iron hoop
3	Bar hole
4	Drumhead
5	Moulding

6	Upper chock
7	Whelp
8	Lower chock
9	Iron staples
10	Iron hoop (partners)
11	Trundlehead
12	Iron spindle
13	Iron stop
14	Iron plate
15	Barrel
16	Quarterdeck
17	Capstan stop
18	Iron hoop
19	Trundlehead
20	Gun deck
21	Drumhead (plan view)

22	Lower end (plan view)
23	Trundlehead (plan view)
24	Lower end (planview)
25	Capstan bar (drumhead)
26	Capstan bar (trundlehead)

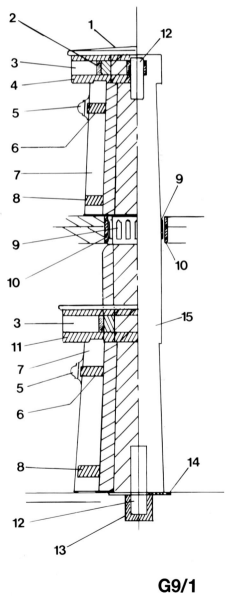

G9/1

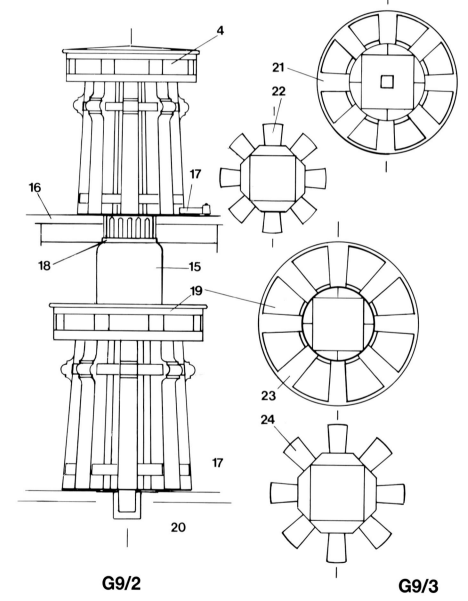

G9/2

G9/3

G9/4

94

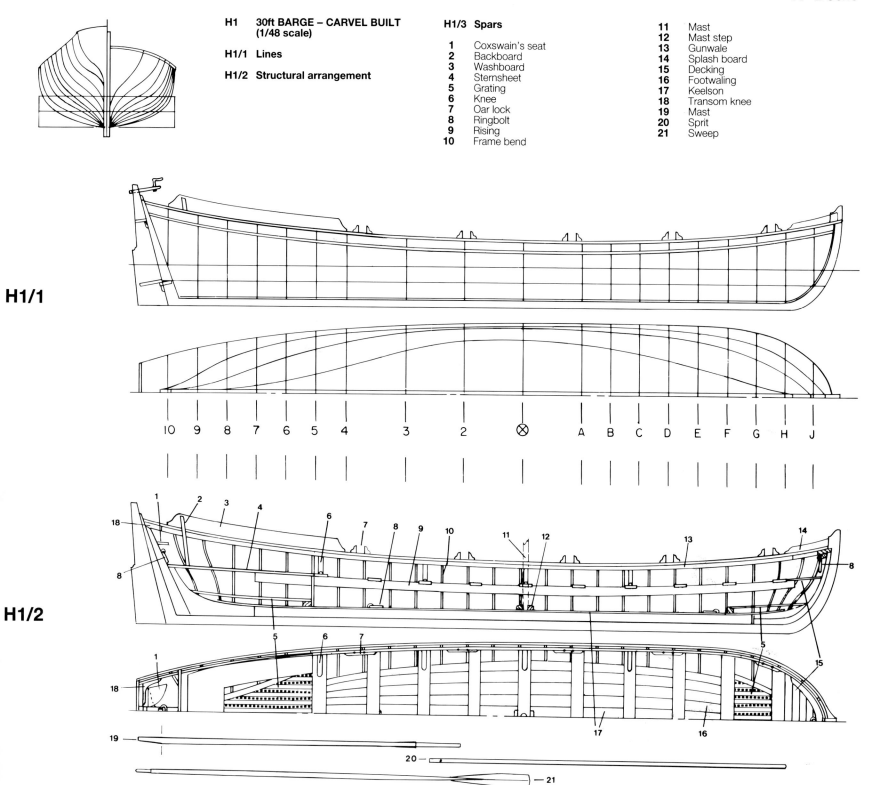

H1 **30ft BARGE – CARVEL BUILT (1/48 scale)**

H1/1 **Lines**

H1/2 **Structural arrangement**

H1/3 **Spars**

1 Coxswain's seat
2 Backboard
3 Washboard
4 Sternsheet
5 Grating
6 Knee
7 Oar lock
8 Ringbolt
9 Rising
10 Frame bend
11 Mast
12 Mast step
13 Gunwale
14 Splash board
15 Decking
16 Footwaling
17 Keelson
18 Transom knee
19 Mast
20 Sprit
21 Sweep

H1/1

H1/2

H1/3

H Boats

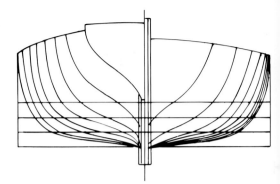

H2   28ft LONGBOAT – CARVEL BUILT
(1/48 scale)

H2/1   Lines

H2/2   Structural arrangement

H2/3   Spars and equipment

1	Davit
2	Sternsheet
3	Footwaling
4	Knee
5	Rowlocks
6	Thwart
7	Windlass
8	Frame bend
9	Mast
10	Mast clamp
11	Gunwale
12	Bowsprit step
13	Bowsprit
14	Grating
15	Footwaling
16	Mast step
17	Iron strap
18	Transom knee
19	Chock
20	Scarf
21	Mainmast
22	Windlass hand spike
23	Driver
24	Sweep
25	Gaff
26	Bowsprit

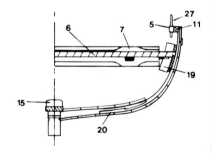

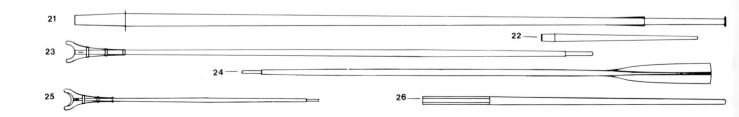

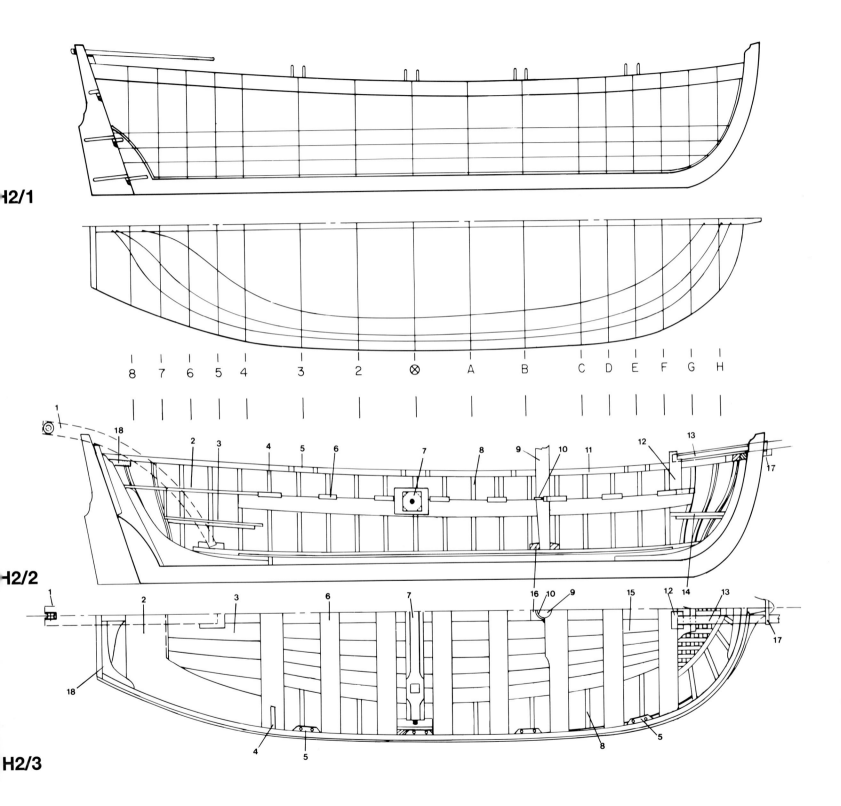

H2/1

8 7 6 5 4 3 2 ⊗ A B C D E F G H

H2/2

H2/3

97

H Boats

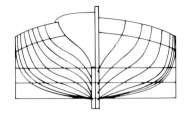

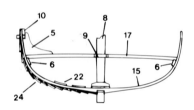

H3/1

H3/2

H3/3

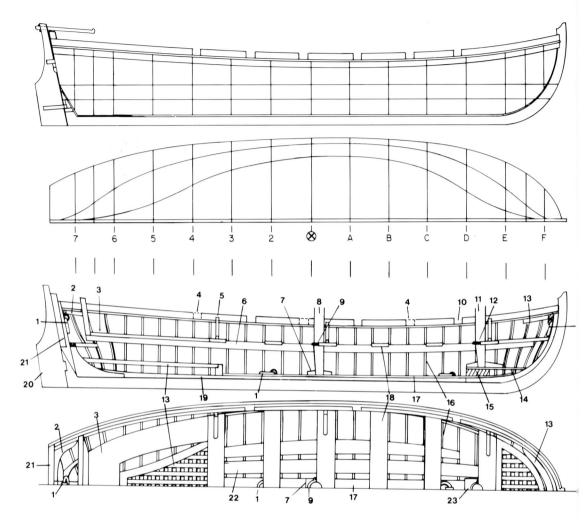

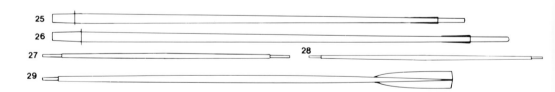

H3   **22ft CUTTER – CLINKER BUILT**
       (1/48 scale)

H3/1   **Lines**

H3/2   **Structural arrangement**

H3/3   **Spars and equipment**

1	Ringbolt
2	Stern knee
3	Sternsheet bench
4	Starboard oarlock
5	Knee
6	Rising
7	Main mast step
8	Main mast
9	Main mast clamp
10	Oarlock
11	Fore mast
12	Fore mast clamp
13	Breast hook
14	Grating
15	Mast chock
16	Frame
17	Keelson
18	Thwart
19	Deadwood
20	Rudder
21	Transom
22	Footwaling
23	Fore mast
24	Step
25	Mainmast

26	Foremast
27	Main yard
28	Fore yard
29	Sweep

H4   18ft YAWL – CARVEL BUILT (1/48 scale)

H4/1   Lines

H4/2   Structural arrangement

H4/3   Spars and equipment

1   Transom
2   Ringbolt
3   Stern knee
4   Sternsheet bench
5   Starboard rowlock
6   Iron knee
7   Frame
8   Riser
9   Mast
10 Rowlock
11 Breasthook
12 Grating
13 Deadwood
14 Mast clamp
15 Mast step
16 Thwart
17 Keelson
18 Deadwood
19 Sprit
20 Sweep
21 Rudder

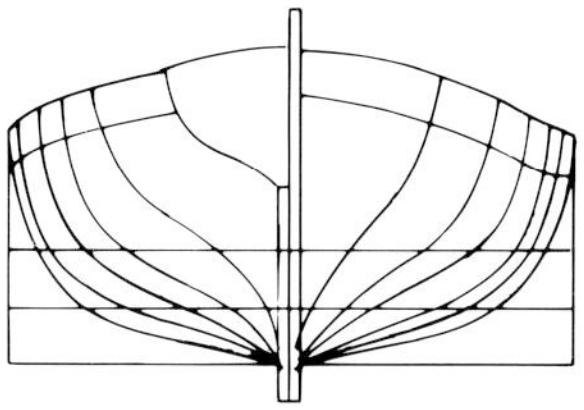

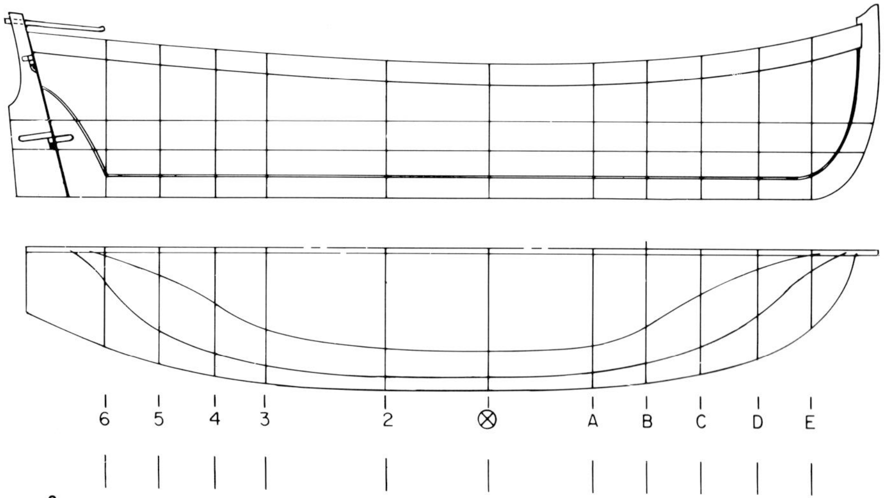

H4/1

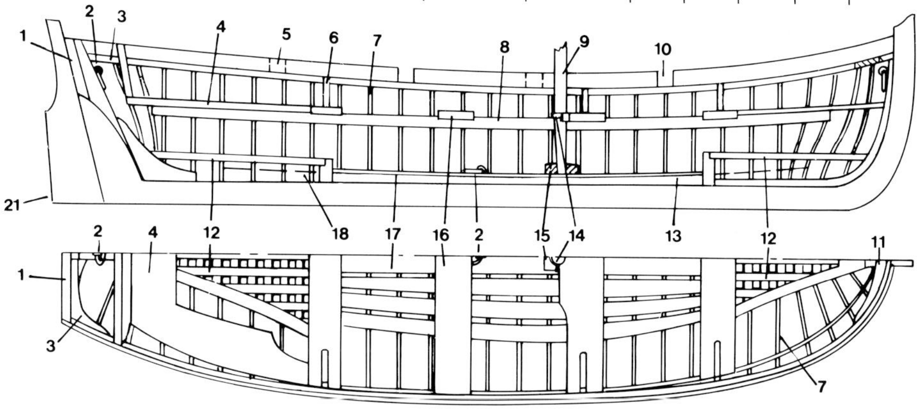

H4/2

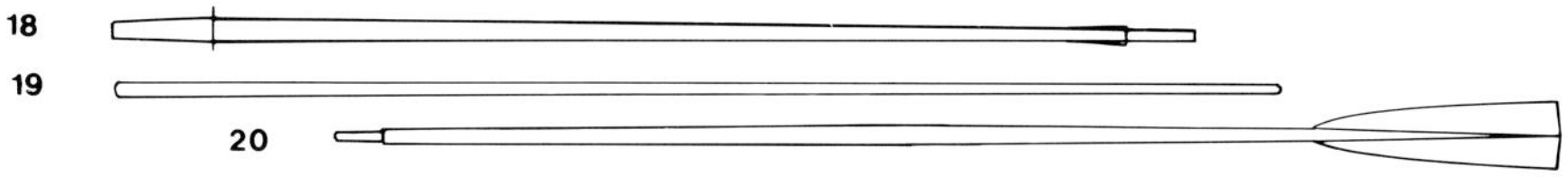

H4/3

J Masts and spars

J1   **LOWER MASTS (1/96 scale)**

J1/1   **Mainmast (starboard side)**

J1/2   **Mainmast (aft side)**

1   Heel
2   Iron hoops
3   Given diameter (partners)
4   Wooldings
5   Cheeks
6   Hounds
7   Battens
8   Front fish and filling
9   Bibs
10   Block
11   Mast tenon

J1/3   **Mast cap**
1   Mast cap viewed from below
2   Mortice for lower mast head
3   Cap (side view)
4   Hole for main topmast
5   Eyebolts

J1/4   **Foremast (starboard side)**

J1/5   **Foremast (aft side)**

J1/6   **Foremast cap (from below and side)**

J1/7   **Mizzen mast (starboard side)**

J1/8   **Mizzen mast (aft side)**

J1/9   **Mizzen mast cap (from below and side)**

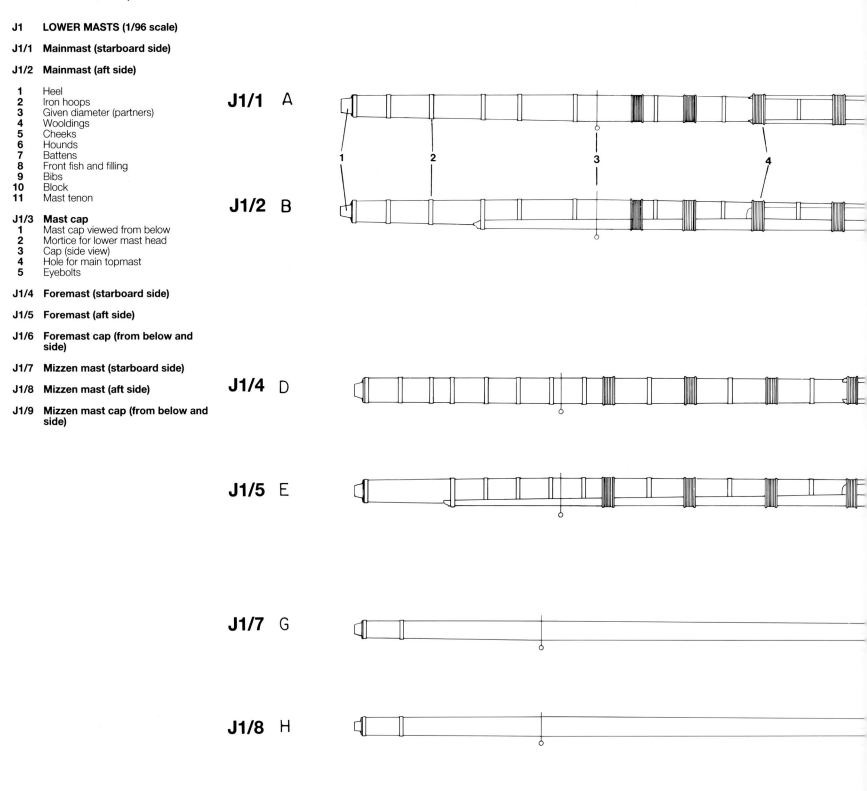

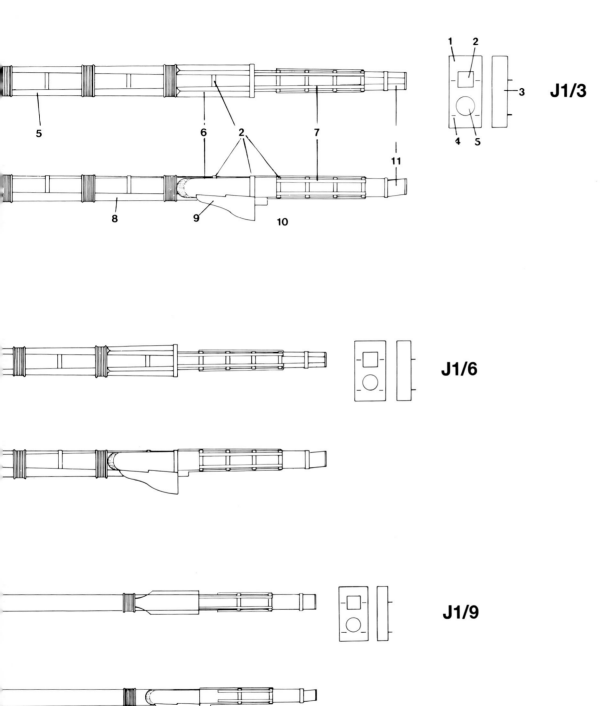

J1/3

J1/6

J1/9

J2

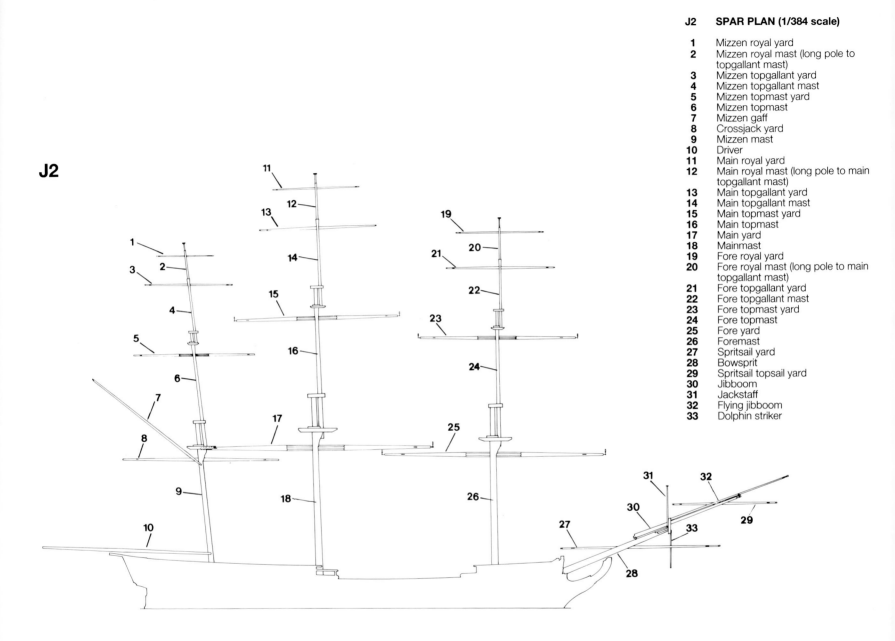

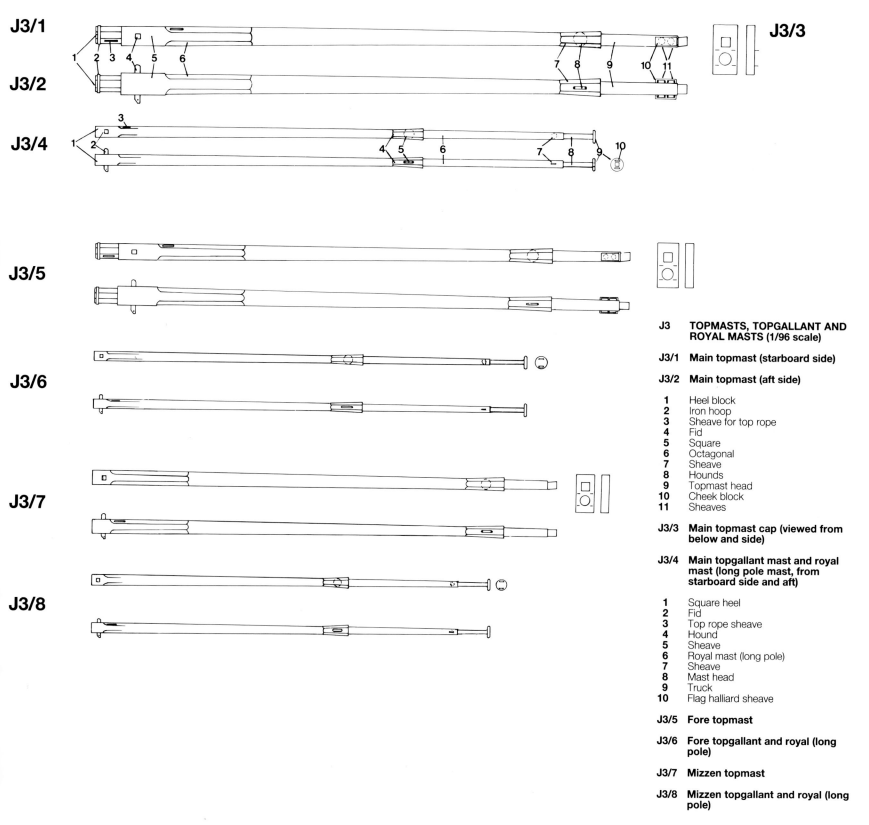

J3/1

1 2 3 4 5 6

J3/2

7 8 9 10 11

J3/3

J3/4

1 2 3 4 5 6 7 8 9 10

J3/5

J3/6

J3/7

J3/8

J3   **TOPMASTS, TOPGALLANT AND ROYAL MASTS (1/96 scale)**

J3/1   **Main topmast (starboard side)**

J3/2   **Main topmast (aft side)**

1   Heel block
2   Iron hoop
3   Sheave for top rope
4   Fid
5   Square
6   Octagonal
7   Sheave
8   Hounds
9   Topmast head
10   Cheek block
11   Sheaves

J3/3   **Main topmast cap (viewed from below and side)**

J3/4   **Main topgallant mast and royal mast (long pole mast, from starboard side and aft)**

1   Square heel
2   Fid
3   Top rope sheave
4   Hound
5   Sheave
6   Royal mast (long pole)
7   Sheave
8   Mast head
9   Truck
10   Flag halliard sheave

J3/5   **Fore topmast**

J3/6   **Fore topgallant and royal (long pole)**

J3/7   **Mizzen topmast**

J3/8   **Mizzen topgallant and royal (long pole)**

J Masts and spars

**J4   BOWSPRIT, JIBBOOM AND
      FLYING JIBBOOM (1/96 scale)**

J4/1   Flying jibboom

1   Tenon
2   Hole for lanyard
3   Octagonal heel
4   Sheave

J4/2   Jibboom

1   Hole for lanyard
2   Sheave
3   Octagonal heel
4   Flying jib bracket

J4/3   Bowsprit

1   Heel tenon
2   Iron hoops
3   Gammoning cleats
4   Fairlead
5   Stop (jibboom)
6   Spritsail collar stop
7   Woolding
8   Bee block
9   Square
10   Bees
11   Sheaves
12   Cap tenon

J4/1

J4/2

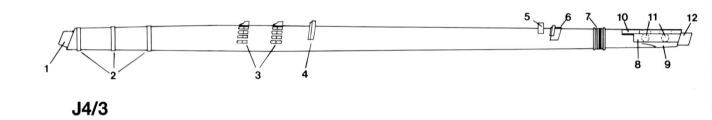

J4/3

J4/4   Bees (plan view) and side view

J4/5   Bowsprit cap (viewed from ahead)

1   Jackstaff
2   Eyebolts
3   Mortice for flying jib
4   Hole for jibboom
5   Mortice for bowsprit tenon
6   Iron straps
7   Dolphin striker
8   Holes
9   Bowsprit cap

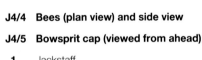

J4/4

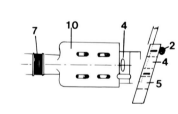

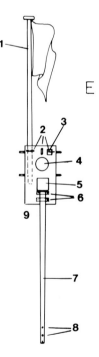

J4/5

J5   DRIVER, GAFF, SPRITSAIL AND SPRITSAIL TOPSAIL YARDS (1/96 scale)

1   Sprig
2   Ferrule
3   Sheave
4   Driver (viewed from above)
5   Iron hoops
6   Jaws
7   Eyebolt
8   Gaff
9   Arm cleat
10   Spritsail yard (viewed from below)
11   Sling cleat
12   Given diameter
13   Spritsail topsail yard (viewed from below)

J5

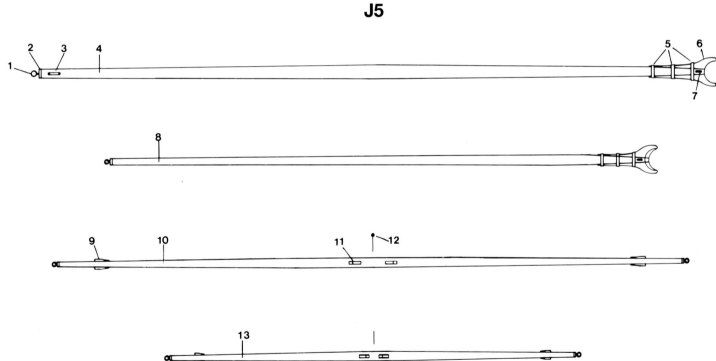

J Masts and spars

J6 **YARDS AND BOOMS (plan views, 1/96 scale)**

J6/1 **Mainmast spars**

J6/2 **Foremast spars**

J6/3 **Mizzenmast spars**

1　Main upper studdingsail yard
2　Given diameter
3　Main swing boom
4　Main lower studdingsail boom
5　Boom brackets
6　Yard battens
7　Yard cleats
8　Lanyard hole
9　Main lower yard
10　Arm cleats
11　Octagonal
12　Upper main topmast studdingsail yard
13　Sling cleats
14　Lower main topmast studdingsail boom
15　Main topmast yard
16　Sheave
17　Upper main topgallant studdingsail yard
18　Topgallant studdingsail boom
19　Sprig
20　Ferrule
21　Main topgallant yard
22　Main royal yard
23　Fore upper studdingsail yard
24　Fore swing boom
25　Fore lower studdingsail boom
26　Fore lower yard
27　Fore topsail studdingsail yard
28　Fore topsail studdingsail boom
29　Fore topsail yard
30　Fore upper topgallant studdingsail yard
31　Fore lower topgallant studdingsail boom
32　Fore royal yard
33　Fore topgallant yard
34　Crossjack yard
35　Mizzen topsail yard
36　Mizzen royal yard
37　Mizzen topgallant yard

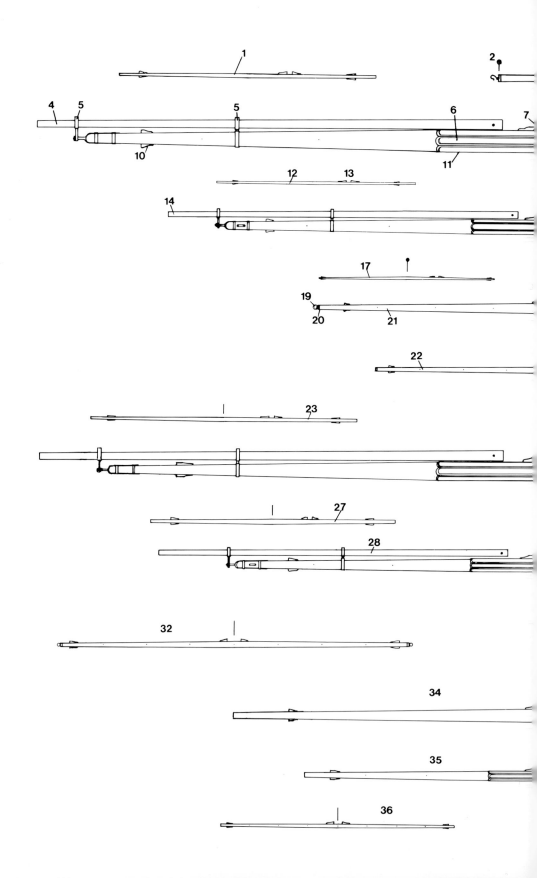

J6/1

J6/2

J6/3

J Masts and spars

J7/1

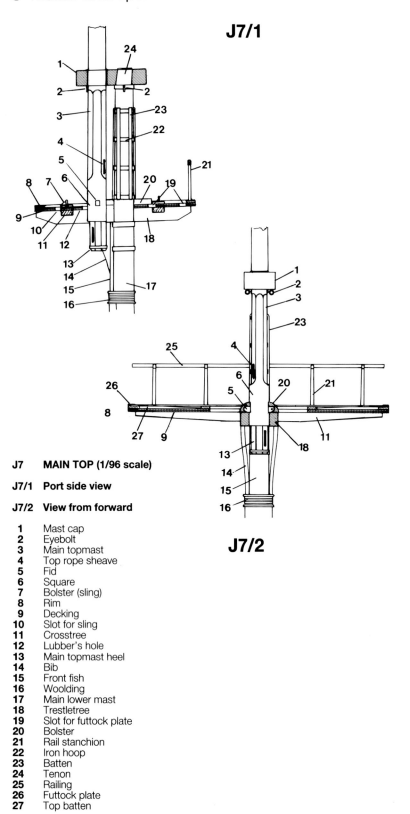

J7 **MAIN TOP (1/96 scale)**

J7/1 **Port side view**

J7/2 **View from forward**

1 Mast cap
2 Eyebolt
3 Main topmast
4 Top rope sheave
5 Fid
6 Square
7 Bolster (sling)
8 Rim
9 Decking
10 Slot for sling
11 Crosstree
12 Lubber's hole
13 Main topmast heel
14 Bib
15 Front fish
16 Woolding
17 Main lower mast
18 Trestletree
19 Slot for futtock plate
20 Bolster
21 Rail stanchion
22 Iron hoop
23 Batten
24 Tenon
25 Railing
26 Futtock plate
27 Top batten

J7/2

J8 **MAINMAST TOPS**

J8/1 **Main topmast top, crosstrees and trestletrees (plan, front and side elevation)**

1 Rabbet for mast head
2 Trestletree (side elevation)
3 Bolster
4 Crosstrees
5 Main topmast head
6 Hole for shroud rope
7 Sheave hole

J8/2 **Main top crosstrees (plan, front, and side elevation)**

J8/3 **Main top trestletrees (plan and side elevation)**

1 Fore sleeper (front elevation)
2 Fore crosstree (plan)
3 Bolt hole
4 Fore crosstree (front elevation)
5 After sleeper (front elevation)
6 After crosstree (plan)
7 Bolt hole
8 After crosstree (front elevation)
9 Bolster

10 Trestletree (side elevation)
11 Rabbet for mast head

J8/4 **Main top (plan view)**

1 Rim (spuce)
2 Decking (pine)
3 Hole for lower yard slings
4 Bolster (lower yard slings)
5 Eyebolt
6 Iron plate let into rim
7 Fore sleeper (plan view)
8 Batten
9 Slot for futtocks
10 Small arms chest (two required)
11 Fid plate
12 Mast block
13 Mainmast head
14 Side batten
15 After sleeper (plan view)
16 Railing plank
17 Mortice for iron stanchion
18 Wood railing
19 Iron stanchion
20 Netting

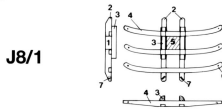

J8/1

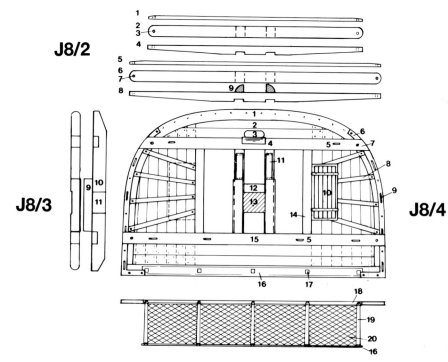

J8/2

J8/3

J8/4

108

J9   FOREMAST TOPS (1/96 scale)

J9/1 Fore topmast top crosstrees and trestletrees (plan, front and side elevation)

J9/2 Fore top crosstrees (plan, front and side elevation)

J9/3 Fore top trestletrees (plan and side elevation)

J9/4 Fore top (plan view)

J10   MIZZEN MAST TOPS (1/96 scale)

J10/1 Mizzen topmast crosstrees and trestletrees (plan, front and side elevation)

J10/2 Mizzen top crosstrees (plan, front and side elevation)

J10/3 Mizzen top trestletrees (plan and side elevation)

J10/4 Mizzen top (plan view)

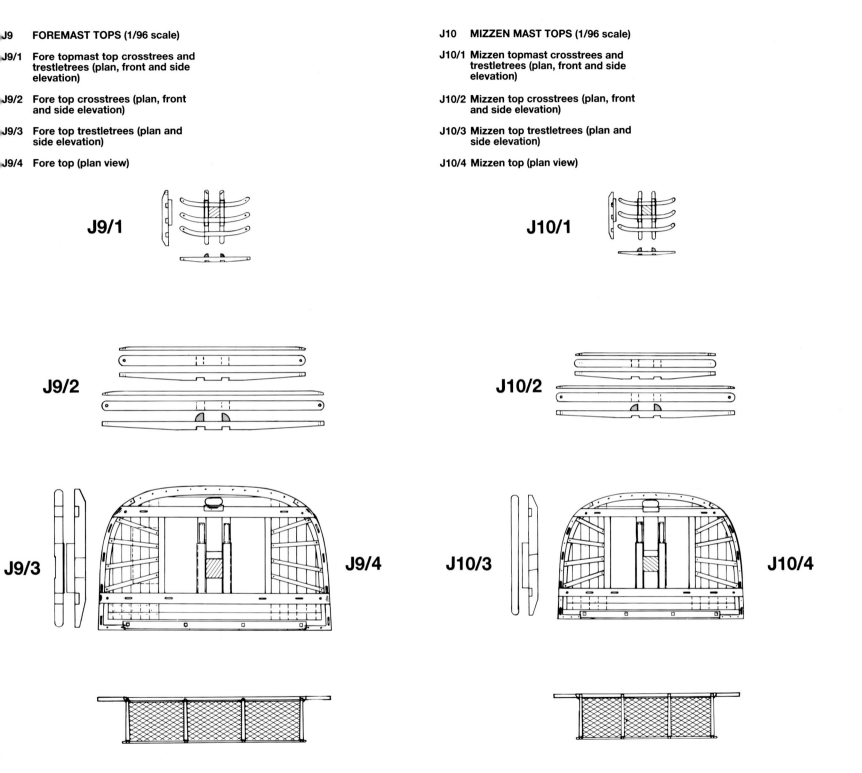

J9/1

J9/2

J9/3

J9/4

J10/1

J10/2

J10/3

J10/4

J11   PERSPECTIVE VIEW OF MAIN
       TOP AND LOWER YARD (no scale)

J11

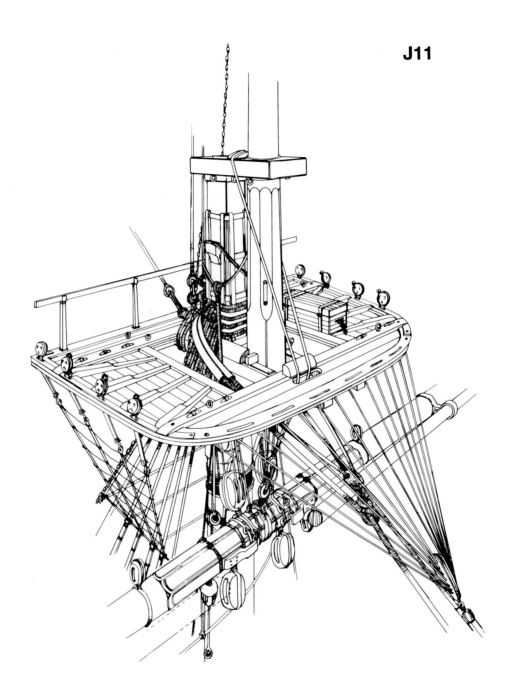

K1 **STANDING RIGGING – SHROUDS**
(1/384 scale)

1   Mizzen topgallant shrouds
2   Mizzen topgallant futtock shrouds
3   Mizzen topmast shrouds
4   mizzen futtock shrouds
5   Mizzen shrouds
6   Main topgallant shrouds
7   Main topgallant futtock shrouds
8   Main topmast shrouds
9   Main futtock shrouds
10 Main shrouds
11 Fore topgallant shrouds
12 Fore topgallant futtock shrouds
13 Fore topmast shrouds
14 Fore futtock shrouds
15 Fore shrouds
16 Fore jib guy
17 Flying jib guy
18 Jib guy
19 Bowsprit shroud
20 Boomkin shroud

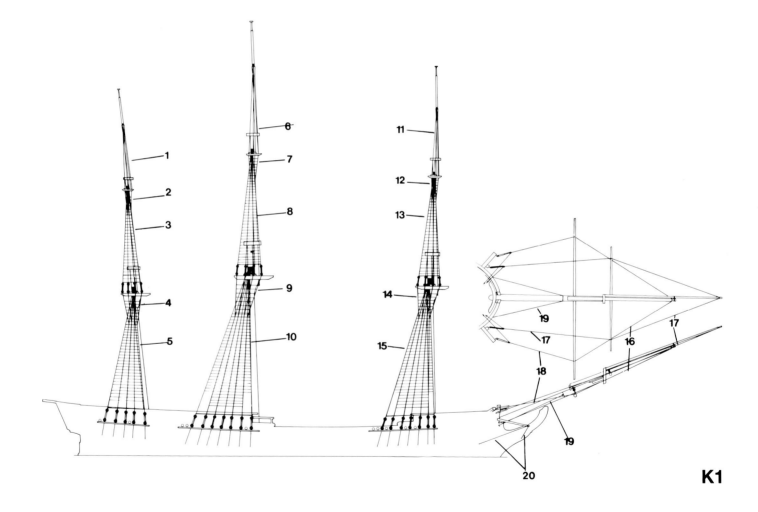

K1

K Sails and rigging

K2

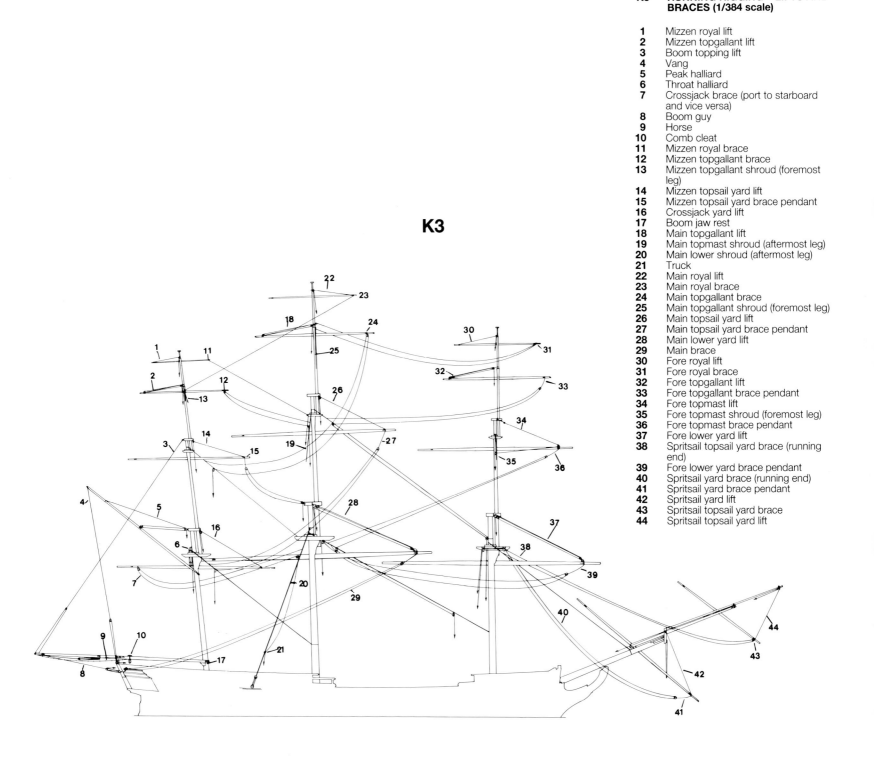

K3

1	Mizzen royal lift
2	Mizzen topgallant lift
3	Boom topping lift
4	Vang
5	Peak halliard
6	Throat halliard
7	Crossjack brace (port to starboard and vice versa)
8	Boom guy
9	Horse
10	Comb cleat
11	Mizzen royal brace
12	Mizzen topgallant brace
13	Mizzen topgallant shroud (foremost leg)
14	Mizzen topsail yard lift
15	Mizzen topsail yard brace pendant
16	Crossjack yard lift
17	Boom jaw rest
18	Main topgallant lift
19	Main topmast shroud (aftermost leg)
20	Main lower shroud (aftermost leg)
21	Truck
22	Main royal lift
23	Main royal brace
24	Main topgallant brace
25	Main topgallant shroud (foremost leg)
26	Main topsail yard lift
27	Main topsail yard brace pendant
28	Main lower yard lift
29	Main brace
30	Fore royal lift
31	Fore royal brace
32	Fore topgallant lift
33	Fore topgallant brace pendant
34	Fore topmast lift
35	Fore topmast shroud (foremost leg)
36	Fore topmast brace pendant
37	Fore lower yard lift
38	Spritsail topsail yard brace (running end)
39	Fore lower yard brace pendant
40	Spritsail yard brace (running end)
41	Spritsail yard brace pendant
42	Spritsail yard lift
43	Spritsail topsail yard brace
44	Spritsail topsail yard lift

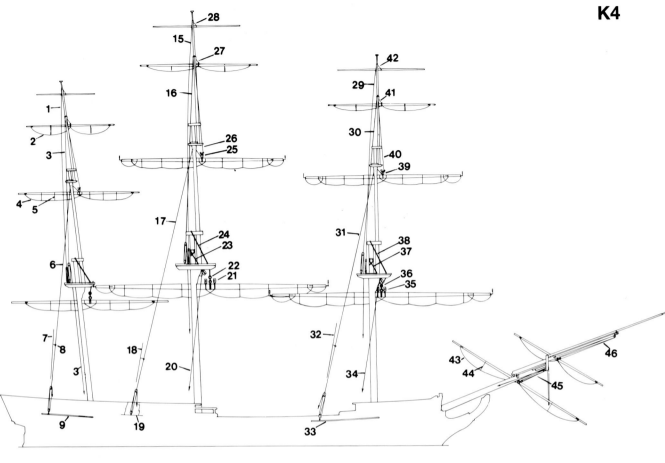

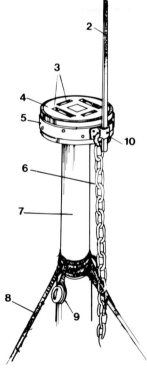

K5

K4	**RUNNING RIGGING – TYES AND HALLIARDS (1/384 scale)**
1	Mizzen royal yard halliard
2	Footrope
3	Mizzen topgallant yard halliard
4	Footrope
5	Stirrup
6	Mizzen topsail yard halliard
7	Mizzen topgallant backstay
8	Bullseye and span
9	Mizzen channel
10	Crossjack yard tye
11	Sling
12	Topsail yard tye
13	Mizzen topgallant yard tye
14	Mizzen royal tye
15	Main royal yard halliard
16	Main topgallant yard halliard
17	Main topsail yard halliard
18	Main topmast backstay
19	Quarterdeck
20	Jeer halliard
21	Jeer block
22	Tye

23	Jeer sling
24	Sling (tye)
25	Main topsail yard tye block
26	Main topsail yard tye
27	Main topgallant yard tye
28	Main royal yard tye
29	Fore royal yard halliard
30	Fore topgallant yard halliard
31	Fore topgallant yard halliard
32	Fore topgallant mast backstay
33	Fore channel
34	Fore jeer halliard
35	Fore jeer block
36	Fore tye
37	Fore lower yard slings (jeer)
38	Fore lower yard slings (tye)
39	Fore topsail yard tye block
40	Fore topsail yard tye
41	Fore topgallant yard tye
42	Fore royal yard tye
43	Spritsail yard footrope
44	Spritsail yard stirrup
45	Spritsail yard halliard
46	Spritsail topsail yard halliard

K5	**LIGHTNING ROD ASSEMBLY (perspective view, no scale)**
1	Silvered tip
2	Copper rod
3	Flag halliard sheaves
4	Mainmast truck
5	Copper strap
6	Conductor chain
7	Main royal mast
8	Main royal backstay
9	Main royal lift block
10	Bracket and ring

K6   SAIL PLAN – SQUARE SAILS
(1/384 scale)

1   Mizzen royal sail
2   Mizzen topgallant sail
3   Mizzen topsail
4   Main royal sail
5   Main topgallant sail
6   Main topsail
7   Main course
8   Fore royal sail
9   Fore topgallant sail
10   Fore topsail
11   Fore course
12   Spritsail
13   Spritsail topsail

K6

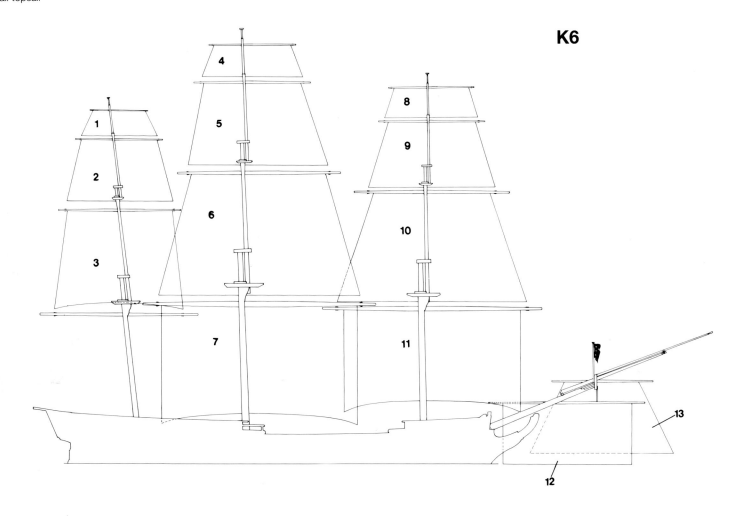

K Sails and rigging

K7 **MIZZEN SQUARE SAILS (1/192 scale)**

K7/1 **Royal sail**

1	Earing
2	Bolt rope
3	Tabling
4	Clew rope

K7/2 **Topgallant sail**

1	Earing
2	Patch
3	Bolt rope
4	Tabling
5	Bowline cringles
6	Lining
7	Clew line

K7/3 **Topsail**

1	Head tabling
2	Earing
3	Reef cringles
4	Leech lining
5	Bowline cringles
6	Clew rope
7	Cloth
8	Bunt line cloth
9	Top lining (aft side)
10	Mast cloth (aft side)
11	Bunt line cringle
12	Foot tabling
13	Middle band
14	Reef bands
15	Holes for reef points
16	Holes for robbands

K7/1

K7/2

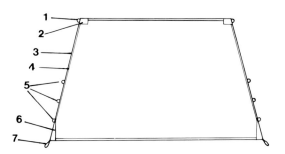

K7/3

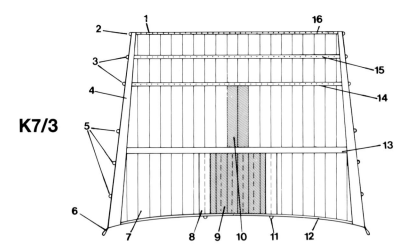

116

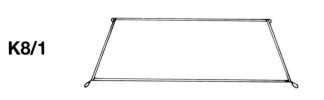

K8/1

K8/2

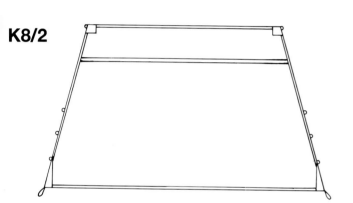

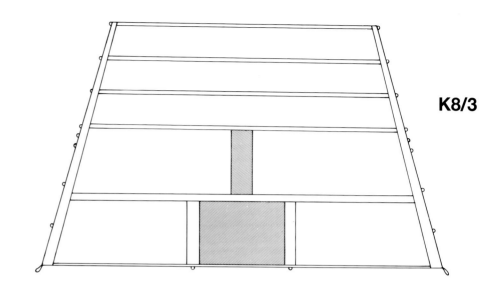

K8/3

K8 **MAIN SQUARE SAILS (fore sides shown, 1/192 scale)**

K8/1 **Royal sail**

K8/2 **Topgallant sail**

K8/3 **Topsail**

K8/4 **Course**

1 Earing
2 Reef cringle
3 Lining
4 Bunt line cringle
5 Clew rope
6 Cloth
7 Bunt line cloths
8 Bunt line cringle
9 Foot tabling
10 Foot bolt rope
11 Leech lining
12 Middle band
13 Reef point holes
14 Reef bands
15 Head tabling
16 Holes for robbands

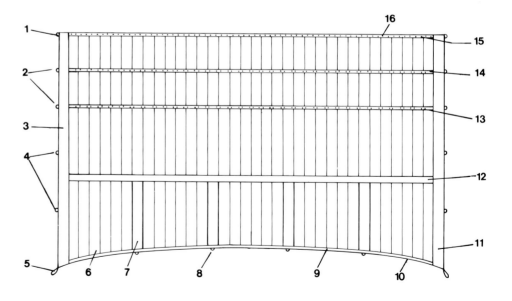

K8/4

K Sails and rigging

K9/1

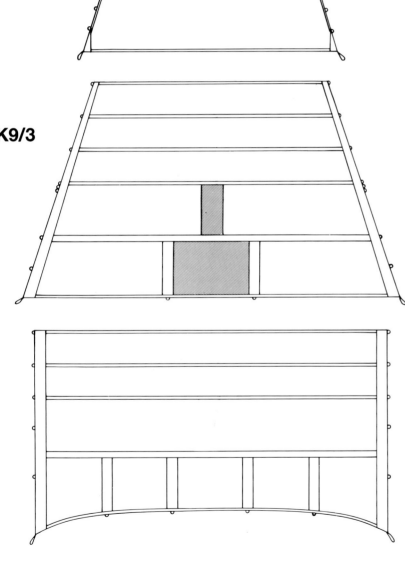

K9 FORE SQUARE SAILS (fore sides shown, 1/192 scale)

K9/1 Royal sail

K9/2 Topgallant sail

K9/3 Topsail

K9/4 Course

K9/2

K9/3

K9/4

K10 SQUARE HEADSAILS (1/192 scale)

K10/1 Spritsail

K10/2 Spritsail topsail

1	Earing
2	Tabling
3	Cloth
4	Bolt rope
5	Reef cringle
6	Water hole
7	Bunt line cringle
8	Holes for reef points
9	Reef band
10	Robband holes

K10/1

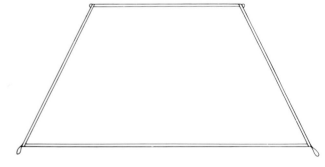

K10/2

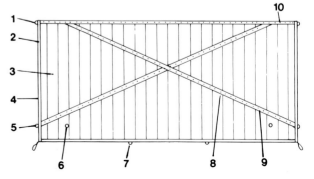

.11 SAIL PLAN – FORE AND AFT
SAILS (1/384 scale)

1 Driver
2 Mizzen royal stay
3 Mizzen topgallant stay
4 Mizzen topgallant staysail
5 Mizzen topmast stay
6 Mizzen topmast staysail
7 Mizzen stay
8 Mizzen staysail
9 Main royal stay
10 Main topgallant stay
11 Main topgallant staysail
12 Main middle stay
13 Main topmast stay
14 Main middle staysail
15 Main topmast staysail
16 Main stay
17 Main staysail
18 Fore topgallant stay
19 Fore jib stay
20 Flying jibsail
21 Fore topmast stay
22 Jibsail
23 Fore topmast staysail
24 Fore stay
25 Fore staysail
26 Ensign
27 Commissioning pennant

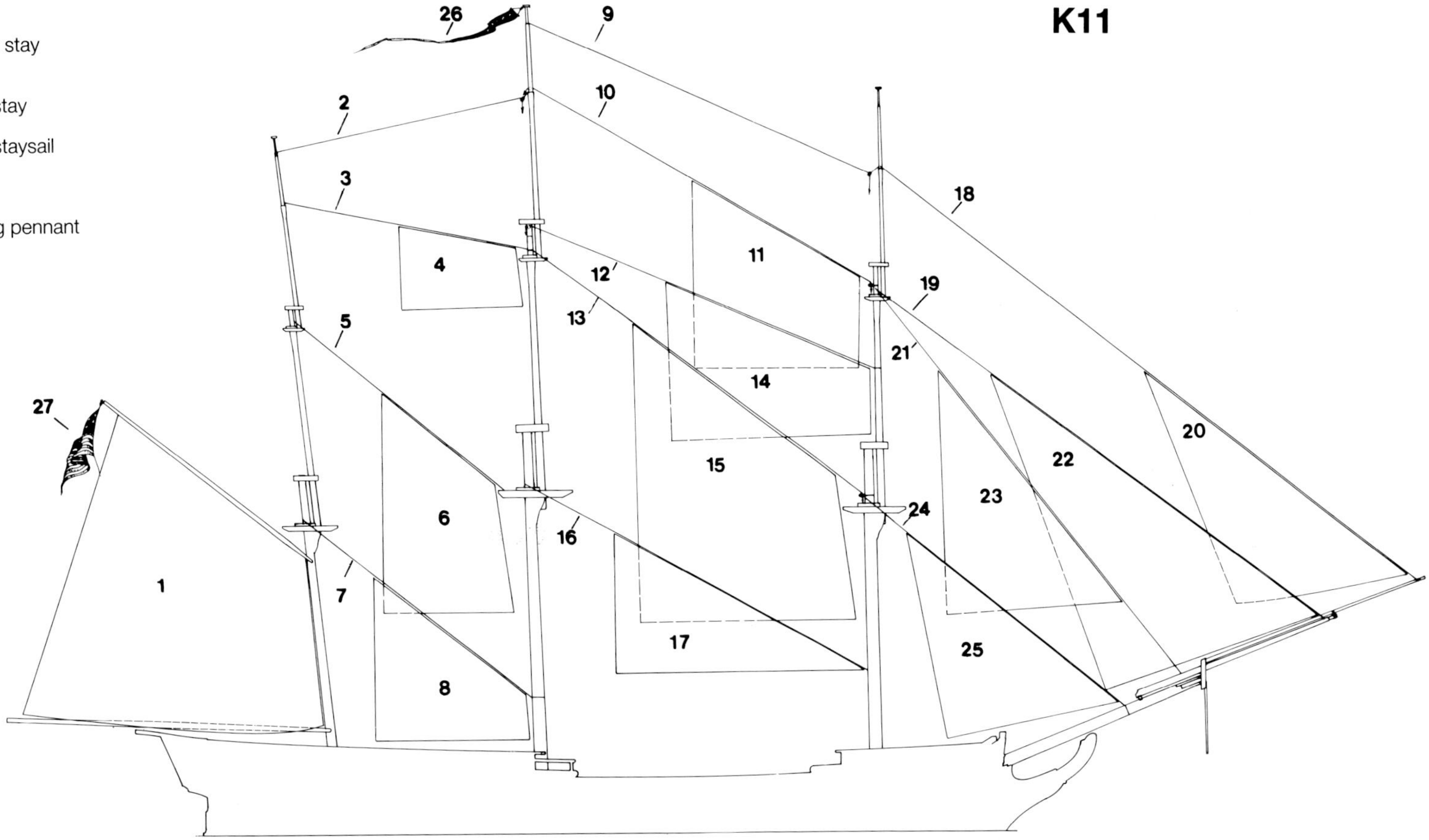

K11

119

K Sails and rigging

K12   MIZZEN FORE AND AFT SAILS
(1/192 scale)

K12/2 Mizzen topgallant staysail

K12/1 Driver

K12/3 Mizzen topmast staysail

K12/4 Mizzen staysail

1   Peak earing thimble
2   Peak piece
3   Brail thimbles
4   Leech bolt rope
5   Lining
6   Reef bands
7   Reef thimbles
8   Clew earing thimble
9   Location of reef points
10   Tabling
11   Tack earing thimble
12   Nock earing thimble
13   Lacing holes
14   Cloth
15   Bolt rope

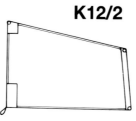

K12/2

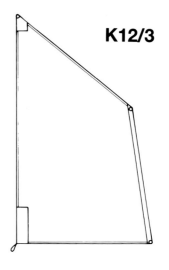

K12/3

K12/1

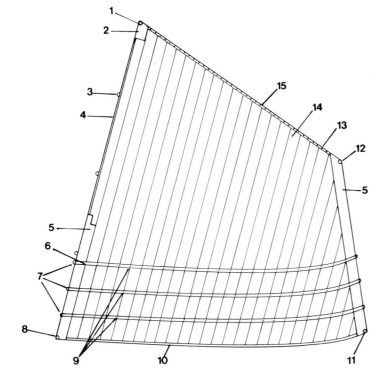

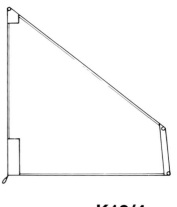

K12/4

K13/1

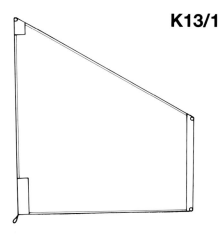

K13/2

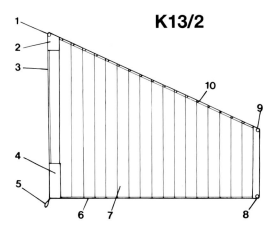

K13 **MAIN FORE AND AFT SAILS**
(1/192 scale)

K13/1 Main topgallant staysail

K13/2 Main middle sail

1	Peak thimble
2	Peak piece
3	Tabling
4	Lining
5	Clew cringle
6	Bolt rope
7	Cloth
8	Tack earing thimble
8	Nock earing thimble
10	Holes fore sail hank lashings

K13/3 Main topsail staysail

1	Main brail cringle

K13/4 Main staysail

K13/3

K13/4

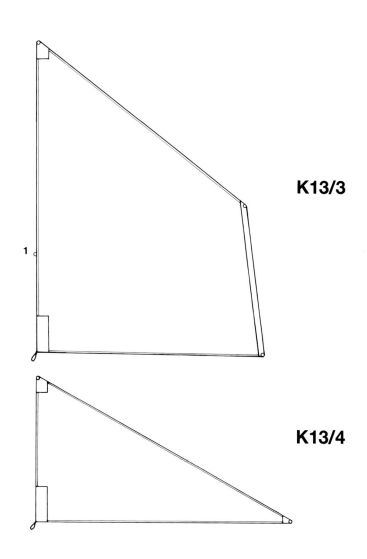

K Sails and rigging

K14   FORE AND AFT HEADSAILS (1/192 scale)

K14/1 Flying jib

K14/2 Jib
1   Peak thimble
2   Bolt rope
3   Tabling
4   Lining
5   Patch
6   Cloth
7   Holes for hank lashings
8   Clew cringle
9   Tack thimble

K14/3 Fore topmast staysail

K14/4 Fore staysail

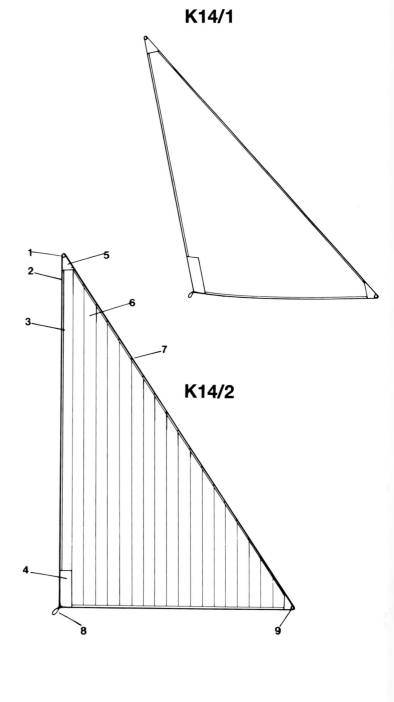

K14/1

K14/2

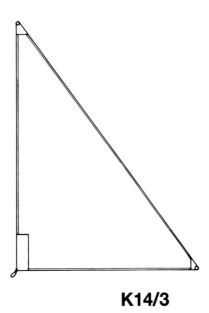

K14/3

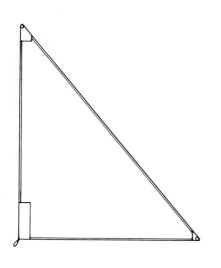

K14/4

K15

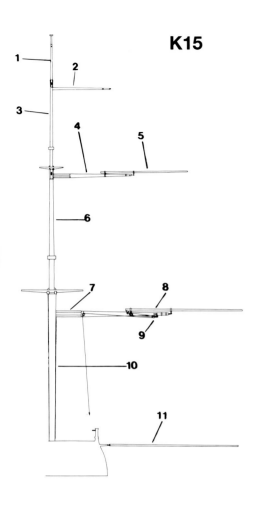

K16 MAIN LOWER STUDDINGSAIL
(1/192 scale)

1	Main masthead cap
2	Main crosstrees
3	Main trestletrees
4	Main lower mast
5	Span at the cap
6	Topping lift (swing boom)
7	Lower main yard
8	Halliard
9	Topping lift pendant
10	Lower studdingsail boom
11	Head earing
12	Swing boom topping lift
13	Gooseneck
14	Fore sheet
15	After sheet
16	Fore guy
17	Block at the side
18	Martingale
19	After guy
20	Thimbles
21	Fore tack
22	After tack
23	Swing boom
24	Foot cringle
25	Tabling
26	Reef band
27	Holes for reef points
28	Lining
29	Holes for head lashing
30	Lower studdingsale yard

K15 MAIN STUDDINGSAIL BOOMS
RUN OUT (1/348 scale)

1	Main royal mast
2	Main topgallant yard
3	Main topgallant mast
4	Main topmast yard
5	Main topmast studdingsail boom
6	Main topmast
7	Main lower yard
8	Main lower studdingsail boom
9	Main lower studdingsail boom tackle
10	Main lower mast
11	Main swing boom

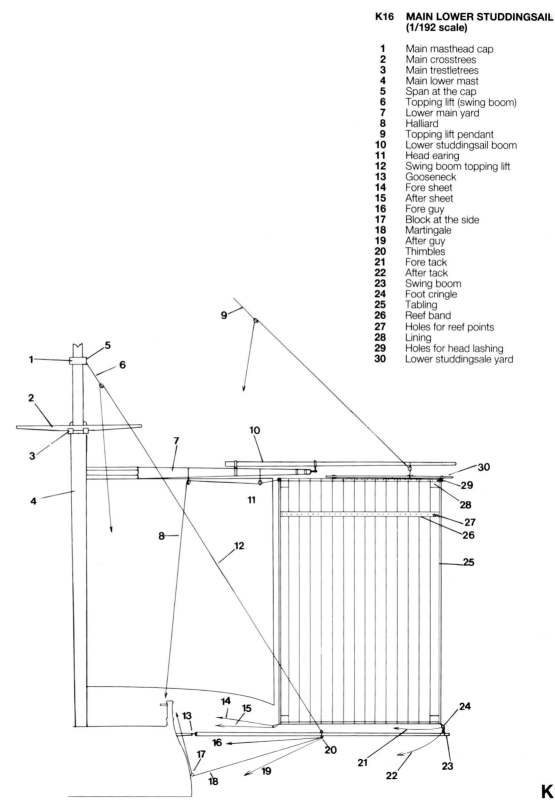

K16

K17

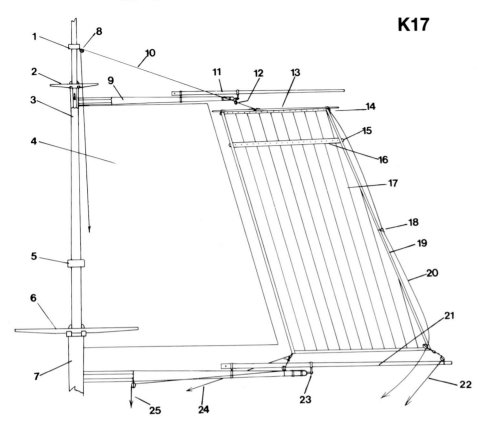

K19

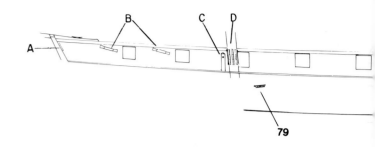

K18 MAIN TOPGALLANT
STUDDINGSAIL (1/192 scale)

1	Main royal mast
2	Studdingsail lift blocks
3	Main topgallant yard
4	Main topgallant sail
5	Main topgallant mast
6	Main topmast cap
7	Main topmast crosstree
8	Main topmast
9	Main topsail yard
10	Main topgallant studdingsail halliard
11	Jewel block
12	Topgallant studdingsail yard
13	Earing cringle
14	Topgallant studdingsail
15	Tabling
16	Clew cringle
17	Thimble
18	Tack
19	Main topmast studdingsail boom
20	Boom iron
21	Fore sheet
22	After sheet

K17 MAIN TOPMAST STUDDINGSAIL
(1/192 scale)

1	Main topmast cap
2	Main topmast crosstree
3	Main topmast
4	Main topsail
5	Main cap
6	Main crosstree
7	Main lower mast
8	Main topmast studdingsail yard lift block
9	Main topmast yard
10	Main topmast studdingsail halliard
11	Main topmast studdingsail boom
12	Jewel block
13	Main topmast studdingsail yard
14	Earing cringle
15	Reef cringle
16	Reef band
17	Main topmast studdingsail
18	Thimble
19	Tabling
20	Downhaul
21	Main yard studdingsail boom
22	Tack
23	Boom iron
24	Fore sheet
25	After sheet
26	Main topsail yard

K19 BELAYING PROFILE (1/192 scale)

A	Taffrail cleats
B	Range cleats
C	Mizzen mast topsail sheet bitts
D	Mizzen mast bitts
E	Main jeer bitts
F	Main mast cleat
G	Main topsail sheet bitts
H	Gangway barricade timberhead
I	Belfry barricade timberhead
J	Fore jeer bitts
K	Fore mast cleats
L	Fore topsail sheet bitts
M	Timberhead
N	Breasthook pin rail
O	Knighthead

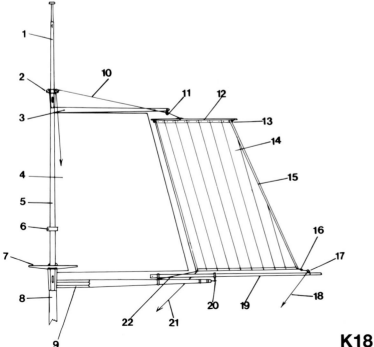

K18

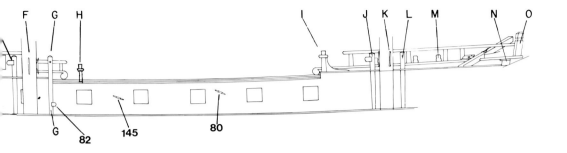

F G H   I   J K L M   N O

G
82   145   80

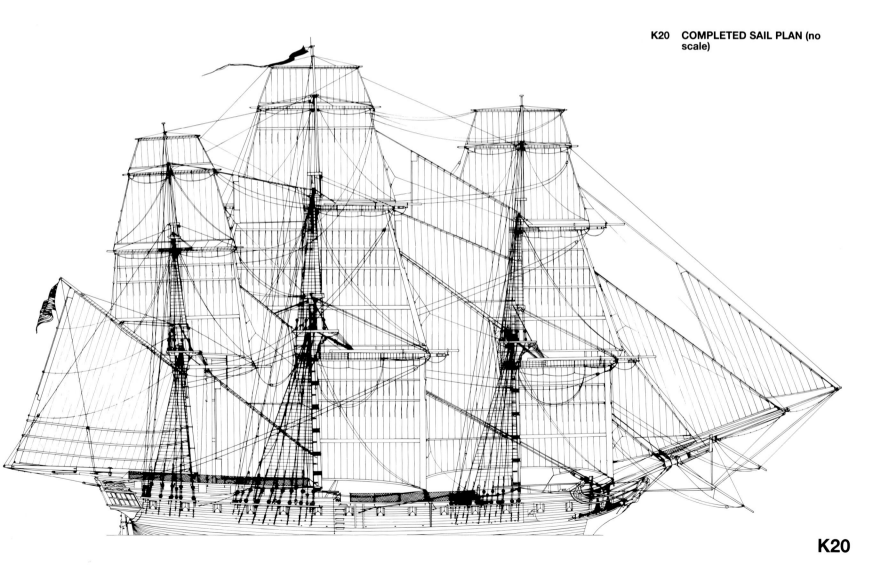

K20   COMPLETED SAIL PLAN (no scale)

K20

K21

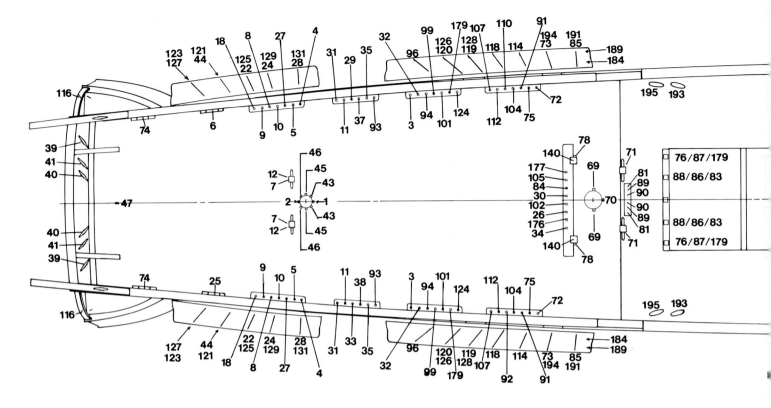

K21 BELAYING PLAN (1/144 scale)

Crossjack
1 Truss pendant
2 Nave line
3 Braces – cross (port to starboard, etc)
4 Lifts

Mizzen topsail
5 Lifts
6 Halliard
7 Braces
8 Clew lines
9 Reef tackles
10 Bunt lines
11 Bowlines
12 Sheets

Mizzen topgallant sail
13 Lifts – mizzen lower top
14 Halliards – mizzen lower top
15 Braces – main lower top
16 Clew lines – mizzen lower top
17 Bowlines – mizzen lower top
18 Sheets

Mizzen royal sail
19 Lifts – mizzen lower top
20 Ties and halliards – mizzen lower top
21 Braces – mizzen lower top
22 Clew lines
23 Bowlines – main lower top
24 Sheets

Mizzen staysail
25 Halliard
26 Downhauler
27 Sheets
28 Brails

Mizzen topmast staysail
29 Halliard
30 Downhauler
31 Sheets
32 Tacks

Mizzen topgallant staysail
33 Halliard
34 Downhauler
35 Sheets
36 Tacks

Driver
37 Throat halliard
38 Peak halliard
39 Vangs
40 Boom sheets
41 Guys
42 Topping lifts – driver boom
43 Peak brails
44 Middle brails
45 Throat brails
46 Foot brails
47 Sheet

Jib
48 Stay
49 Halliard

50 Downhaler-inhauler (for traveller)
51 Sheets
52 Tacks
53 Outhauler

Flying jib
54 Stay
55 Halliard
56 Downhauler-inhauler (for traveller)
57 Sheets
58 Tacks – made fast at jibboom

Spritsail
59 Braces
60 Lifts
61 Bunt lines
62 Clew lines
63 Sheets

Spritsail topsail
64 Braces
65 Lifts
66 Bunt lines
67 Clew lines
68 Sheets

Main course
69 Truss pendants
70 Nave line
71 Jeers
72 Outer tricing lines
73 Inner tricing lines
74 Braces
75 Lifts

76 Leech lines
77 Bunt lines
78 Clew garnets
79 Sheets – cleat gun deck
80 Tacks – cleat gun deck
81 Bowlines
82 Slab lines

Main topsail
83 Lifts
84 Halliards
85 Braces
86 Clew lines
87 Reef tackles
88 Bunt lines
89 Bowlines
90 Sheets

Main topgallant sail
91 Lifts
92 Halliards
93 Braces
94 Clew lines
95 Bowlines – main lower top
96 Sheets

Main royal sail
97 Braces – main lower top
98 Lifts – main lower top
99 Clew lines
100 Bowlines – main lower top
101 Sheets

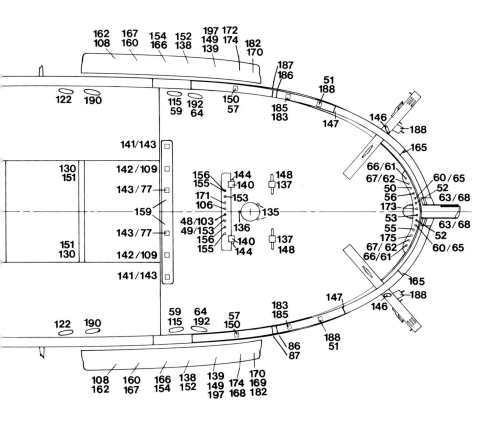

Main staysail
102 Halliard
103 Downhauler
104 Sheets

Main topmast staysail
105 Halliard
106 Downhauler
107 Sheets
108 Tacks
109 Brails

Main topgallant staysail
110 Halliard
111 Downhauler – fore lower top
112 Sheets
113 Tacks – fore lower top

Main studdingsail
114 Topping lift
115 Fore guy
116 After guy
117 Martingale – main channel
118 Outer halliard
119 Inner halliard
120 Fore tack
121 After tack
122 Fore sheet
123 After sheet

Main topmast studdingsail
124 Topping lift
125 Brace
126 Halliard

127 Tack
128 Fore sheet
129 After sheet
130 Downhauler

Main topgallant studdingsail
131 Halliard
132 Tack – main channel, as convenient
133 Fore sheet å- made fast to yard
134 After sheet – main lower top

Fore course
135 Truss pendants
136 Nave line
137 Jeers
138 Outer tricing lines
139 Inner tricing lines
140 Braces
141 Lifts
142 Leech lines
143 Bunt lines
144 Clew garnets
145 Sheets – cleat gun deck
146 Tacks
147 Bowlines
148 Slablines

Fore topsail
149 Lifts
150 Halliards
151 Braces
152 Clew lines
153 Reef tackles
154 Bunt lines

155 Bowlines
156 Sheets

Fore topgallant sail
157 Lifts – fore lower top rail
158 Halliards – fore lower top
159 Braces
160 Clew lines
161 Bowlines
162 Sheets

Fore royal sail
163 Braces
164 Lifts
165 Bowlines
166 Clew lines
167 Sheets

Fore staysail
168 Halliard
169 Downhauler
170 Sheets

Fore topmast staysail
171 Stay
172 Halliard
173 Downhauler
174 Sheets
175 Outhauler

Middle staysail
176 Stay
177 Halliard
178 Downhauler

179 Sheets
180 Tacks – fore lower top
181 Tricing line – fore lower top

Fore studdingsail
182 Topping lift
183 Fore guy
184 After guy
185 Martingale
186 Outer halliard
187 Inner halliard
188 Fore tack
189 After tack
190 Fore sheet
191 After sheet

Fore topmast studdingsail
192 Topping lift
193 Brace
194 Halliard
195 Tack
196 Fore sheet – fore top shroud
197 After sheet
198 Downhauler

Fore topgallant studdingsail
199 Halliard – fore lower top rail
200 Tack – fore lower top
201 Fore sheet – fore lower top
202 After sheet – lashed to yard